SpringerBriefs in Business

For further volumes:
http://www.springer.com/series/8860

Ali Anari • James W. Kolari

Excel-Based Business Analysis

Forecasting Key Business Trends

 Springer

Ali Anari
Texas A&M University
Mays Business School
College Station, TX 77843, USA
manari@mays.tamu.edu

James W. Kolari
Texas A&M University
Mays Business School
College Station, TX 77843, USA
jkolari@mays.tamu.edu

ISSN 2191-5482   e-ISSN 2191-5490
ISBN 978-1-4614-2049-1   e-ISBN 978-1-4614-2050-7
DOI 10.1007/978-1-4614-2050-7
Springer New York Dordrecht Heidelberg London

Library of Congress Control Number: 2011941444

Printed on acid-free paper

Springer is part of Springer Science+Business Media (www.springer.com)

Disclaimer

The authors and Springer assume no responsibility for any errors that may appear in this manual or the excel programs. The programs are provided as is without any guarantees or warranty. Although the authors have attempted to find and correct any bugs in the free software programs, the authors are not responsible for any damage or losses of any kind caused by the use or misuse of the programs. The authors are under no obligation to provide support, service, corrections, or upgrades to the free software programs. The user assumes all responsibility for the selection of the program to achieve intended results, and for the installation, use, and results obtained from the programs.

Preface

"The trend is your friend" is a practical principle often used by business managers. Managers seek to forecast their future sales, expenditures, and profitability in order to make production and other operational decisions. The problem is how best to identify and discover business trends and utilize trend information for attaining objectives of firms.

This book contains an Excel-based solution to this problem. A more in-depth book by the authors entitled *The Power of Profit* by Springer (2009) proposed a "profit system model" of the firm that enables forecasts of trends in sales, expenditures, profits, and other business variables. Here, we are pleased to provide an Excel version of the profit system model that is easy to use and should make our model available to a wider audience of potential users for detecting and estimating business trends. For those who are more sophisticated in statistical analysis, standard econometric packages can also be used.

Our Excel solution is conveniently provided in a computer program dubbed *FIRM* to be run on Windows with Microsoft Excel 2010. *FIRM* can be used to forecast trends in the following key business variables: sales, assets, profits, profit rate, and profit margin for conventional (unregulated profit) firms. The program uses historical time series of total sales, total costs, and total assets of the firm from its financial statements (income statements and balance sheets); estimates relationships among these variables; and then employs the estimated relationships to forecast trends in these vital business variables. Our goal is to equip business managers and students with easy-to-use tools for both understanding and forecasting trends in important business variables, thereby empowering them to make better business decisions.

Learning by Example

This book allows users to "learn by example" based on historical financial data for an actual US firm. To demonstrate how to use the business analysis program *FIRM*, historical time series of total sales, total costs, and total assets are provided for the building supply company Home Depot.

Business Modeling and Simulation as a Learning Process

Ezra Solomon, a member of President Nixon's Council of Economic Advisors, once said: "The only function of economic forecasting is to make astrology look respectable." Despite its past records, economic forecasts are made formally or informally by business and government organizations in an effort to find the most probable alternative futures resulting from current decisions. The issue of economic forecasting is not whether or not to forecast, but how to utilize all available information efficiently as inputs for the output of finding alternative futures. Although economic models have not been highly successful for forecasting short-term fluctuations in economic and business variables, time series economic and business models have been more successful in forecasting trends in business variables over longer periods. Time series models of firms and industries can use past histories of the most fundamental business variables and the relationships among these variables to extract long-term trends in business data—more specifically, to discover the average paths of expected values of business variables.

Annual statements of firms' balance sheets and income statements contain their past records of revenues (sales), profits, capital stocks, and labor employed to produce goods and services. Organizing these records based on annual or quarterly data gives time series of these variables. Anari and Kolari (2009) show that there are dynamic relationships among sales, assets, profit, profit rate, and profit margin and that these relationships can be exploited using equations for these fundamental business variables. The resultant model of the firm can be estimated and then be used for forecasting business trends as well as simulation of business decisions. Thus, our profit system model of the firm is an analytical framework to organize business data variables to learn about the relationships among the variables. By comparing the forecasts of business trends generated from the model *FIRM* with actual outcomes of key variables, the learning process is expected to help model users to utilize productively the information contained in accounting information for forecasting and business decision making.

What You Should Know to Use This Book

Users need to install the Analysis Toolpak, an Excel add-in program that is available when Microsoft Office or Excel is installed. To install the Analysis Toolpak, choose the Office Button, then select Excel Options, then select Add-Ins, and finally select Analysis Toolpak VBA. Also, the Excel Ribbon should display the Developer tab in order to run *FIRM*. To show the Developer tab for Microsoft Office 2010 applications, (1) click the File tab, (2) click Options, (3) click Customize Ribbon, (4) select Developer, and (5) click OK to close the Options dialog box. To show the Developer tab for Excel 2007, (1) click the Microsoft

Office Button, (2) click Excel Options, (3) click Popular, and (4) select the Show Developer tab in the Ribbon check box.

Only everyday Excel tasks such as Copy, Paste, and Delete are needed to use the model *FIRM*. Also, users can utilize the time series data produced by the programs to draw charts, compute moving averages of the time series, and compute various statistics such as mean and standard deviation.

How to Use the Excel Software in This Book

The user familiar with Excel can begin with Chap. 3, use the software with the supplied time series data for Home Depot, and by means of only a few clicks, see the forecasts of trends in sales, assets, and profits and perform some simulations. Of course, those interested to know more about the foundations of the model of the firm can read our 2009 book *The Power of Profit*. For those familiar with econometrics, our Excel programs can be used as a prelude to using econometric packages to develop profit system models as discussed in *The Power of Profit*.

System Requirements

To use this book's program, a copy of Microsoft Excel 2007 or later versions needs to be installed on your computer.

Support Information

We have made every effort to ensure the accuracy of examples in this book and the programs contained in the companion disk. To provide feedback on the programs and the book's contents, you can send email to: Manari@mays.tamu.edu or Jkolari@mays.tamu.edu.

College Station, TX, USA   Ali Anari
                                                                                       James W. Kolari

Acknowledgments

Special thanks are extended to Nicholas Philipson, who is our editor on this project. His encouragement and faithful support of our profit system model ideas are most appreciated.

About the Authors

Dr. Ali Anari obtained his PhD in Industrial Economics and Business Studies at the University of Birmingham, UK, in 1978. He has more than 30 years research experience in developing computer-based economic models for economic analysis and forecasting in the areas of business economics, macroeconomics, real estate economics, and regional economics. In his professional career Dr. Anari has been a research economist in the areas of national and regional economic modeling at the Real Estate Research Center for Business and Economic Analysis in the Mays Business School at Texas A&M University; Visiting Scholar in the Anderson School of Management of the University of California, Los Angeles; research economist at the Imperial College of Science and Technology, London; research fellow at the University of Birmingham, UK; and economic analyst at the Economics and Statistics Department of National Iranian Oil Company. He has presented papers on economic modeling at conferences around the world and published book chapters and articles in such scholarly publications as the *Journal of Money, Credit, and Banking*, *Journal of Applied Economics*, *Journal of Financial Research*, *Journal of Real Estate Economics*, *Journal of Economics and Business*, *Journal of Energy Policy*, and *Journal of Emerging Markets*. Current research interests include the relationship between inflation and interest rates, economic models for early warning of real estate bubbles, the role of profitability in economic growth, and regional profitability analysis.

Prof. James W. Kolari obtained his PhD in Finance at Arizona State University in 1980 and thereafter has taught financial markets and institutions at Texas A&M University in the Finance Department. In 1994 he was awarded the JPMorgan Chase Professorship in Finance in the Mays Business School. He has more than 30 years research experience in the areas of computer-based modeling of financial markets (including stock, bond, and real estate markets), financial institutions (such as banks and insurance companies), and financial regulation. Over the years, he has been a Visiting Scholar at the Federal Reserve Bank of Chicago, Fulbright Scholar at the University of Helsinki and Bank of Finland, Faculty Fellow with the Mortgage Bankers Association of America, and Senior Research Fellow at the

Swedish School of Business and Economics (Hanken) in Finland, in addition to being a consultant to the US Small Business Administration, US Information Agency, American Bankers Association, Independent Bankers Association of America, and numerous banks and other organizations. He has published over 100 articles in refereed journals, numerous other papers and monographs, and 12 coauthored books. His papers have appeared in such domestic and international journals as the *Journal of Finance*, *Review of Financial Studies*, *Journal of Business*, *Journal of Money, Credit and Banking*, *Journal of Economic Dynamics and Control*, *Journal of Banking and Finance*, *Real Estate Economics*, *Journal of International Money and Finance*, and *Scandinavian Journal of Economics*. Papers in Dutch, Finnish, Italian, Swedish, and Russian have appeared outside of the USA. He is a coauthor of leading college textbooks in commercial banking and international business courses.

Contents

Chapter 1
Introduction

Abstract This chapter introduces a model of the firm dubbed *FIRM* for business forecasting and analysis. The model consists of equations for fundamental business variables, including sales, total costs, total assets, total profits, profit rate, and profit margin. Input data required to run the model consist of time series of total costs, total sales, and total assets. The model estimates the business equations and generates forecasts of business variables. The model can also be used for simulation of profit planning, investment evaluation, and stock analysis of corporations.

Keywords Model of the firm • Fundamental business variables • Business forecasting • Business simulations

Whether a Fortune 500 corporation or a small corner shop, on a day-to-day basis, management must make decisions about fundamental business variables such as sales, costs, assets, profit rate, and profit margin. In our book entitled *The Power of Profit* (2009), we show that dynamic relationships among these variables can be expressed in terms of equations to develop a *profit system model* of the firm that can be estimated from the historical data for these variables using regression analysis. Importantly, the estimated model can then be used for forecasting trends in these key business variables.

To make it easy for managers to implement our profit system model, in this book we provide an Excel-based program named *FIRM* for estimating the relationships among sales, profits, and costs of business activities. The program is useful not only for forecasting purposes, but also for simulation of the probable paths of the fundamental business variables. With regard to the latter, the estimated model can be used for simulating the probable outcomes of alternative profit planning strategies (e.g., cost reduction), capital budgeting, and investment strategies. The Excel program equips business managers with tools for better understanding and forecasting their business operations and for making better decisions.

A. Anari and J.W. Kolari, *Excel-Based Business Analysis: Forecasting Key Business Trends*, SpringerBriefs in Business 8, DOI 10.1007/978-1-4614-2050-7_1,
© Ali Anari and James W. Kolari 2012

1.1 A Model of the Firm

We model the firm using a set of equations for sales, capital stocks, costs, profits, profit rate, and profit margin. These equations comprise the profit system model for business analysis. By estimating this equation system, you can obtain the probable paths of these variables in the future that are expected to occur in view of today's managerial decisions.

Annual accounting statements of firms contain data and information on the current and past magnitudes of sales, costs, profits, and assets of firms. Organizing this historical accounting data on an annual or quarterly basis gives historical time series for these variables which can be used for estimating their relationships using regression analysis methods. The profit system model of the firm presented in the next chapter is an analytical tool for organizing these historical time series and summarizing the information contained in these historical time series variables in the form of equations.

The program *FIRM* is designed for the business analysis of conventional firms (unregulated, profit-oriented firms). The model consists of equations for total sales, capital stocks, profit rate, profit margin, total profit, and total costs of the firm in a period. Equations for total sales, total assets, and profit rate are regression equations estimated by ordinary least squares method. Equations for profit margin, total profits, and total costs are then estimated from these three estimated equations. Program *FIRM* uses the time series of total sales, total costs, and total assets and produces:

- Regression equations for total sales, total assets, and profit rate
- Forecasts of total sales, total assets, total costs, total profits, profit rate, and profit margin and
- A simulation model of the firm containing the dynamic relationships among sales, assets, costs, profits, profit rate, and profit margin for the analysis of the probable paths of these business variables in the future in response to today's managerial decisions

Only a basic understanding of Excel is needed, as we give step-by-step instructions on how to run the model *FIRM*. For those who are experienced econometricians or statistical analysts, we recommend using econometric modeling packages, such as *Eviews7*, that can include more variables in the models and utilize more sophisticated econometric techniques.

1.2 Simulations of Model *FIRM*

The program *FIRM* has an Excel worksheet for simulation of the impact of changes in initial conditions for total costs, total sales, and total assets on the expected future values of these variables in addition to the future values of total profit, profit rate, and profit margin. The program allows the simulation of the probable outcomes of alternative managerial decisions for investment, capital budgeting, profit planning, and stock market analysis of corporations.

Investment evaluation and capital budgeting. Fixed investments in land, buildings, and equipment are normally costly, subject to uncertainty, and difficult to reverse if they later turn out to be unsuccessful. New additions to existing capital stocks or abandonment of unworthy existing economic activities can generate changes in the sequential capital accumulation path which may result in suboptimal trajectories of sales, assets, costs, profits, profit rates, and profit margins over long periods of time. Although the expected profit rate or the net present value of benefits or profits of individual projects may look initially favorable, the cumulative path of the benefits or profits as time passes may prove to be smaller than expected.

Simulations of the estimated model generate the expected sequential paths of sales, assets, total profits, profit rates, profit margins, and total costs resulting from changes in the initial conditions of these fundamental business variables. Comparisons of the simulated paths for costs and benefits with respect to the outcomes of alternative investment decisions provide critical information for investment evaluation and capital budgeting decisions.

Profit planning. Managerial decisions affecting the firm's total costs, pricing, sales volume, investments in new capital stocks, and abandonment of existing activities in a period are expected to impact the future trajectories of sales, capital stocks, costs, profits, profit rates, and profit margins due to the dynamic relationships among these variables. The model *FIRM* presented in this book are designed for simulating and estimating the paths of these key business variables due to changes in prices, costs, and quantities of goods.

Stock market analysis of corporations. For corporations, discounting the time series of a firm's profits by an appropriate discount rate gives the trajectory of market valuation for the firm. Dividing the time series of a firm's total profits by the time series of the number of shares outstanding gives profit per share. Dividing profit per share by an appropriate discount rate yields the time series of the equity market values of the corporation. The model *FIRM* enables projections of profit which can be used in estimating stock values for firms.

1.3 Closing Remarks

This book and its companion software fit into the general fields of managerial economics or business analysis. These areas use the disciplines of microeconomic theory and management decision science in order to find the most probable alternative futures resulting from current decisions by firms. In our book *The Power of Profit*, we show that the profit system model can be applied to individual firms, a group of firms, industries, and the whole business sector. The Excel-based model *FIRM* in this book opens up its ready usage by managers in conventional (unregulated profit) firms. Ultimately, it is our hope that the Excel program *FIRM* will contribute to better decision making, higher profits, and improved management by business firms.

Chapter 2
A Business Simulation Model of Conventional Firms

Abstract This chapter discusses an accounting approach for the derivation of our business model *FIRM* from the concepts of profit rate and profit margin. Equations for fundamental business variables are presented, including sales, assets, total costs, total profit, profit rate, and profit margin. A system equations approach is discussed for estimating these equations by means of regression methods for the purposes of business analyses and simulations.

Keywords Regression equations • System equation approach • Sales equation • Profit rate equation • Capital stocks equation • Profit margin equation

As discussed in Chap. 1, our profit system model of the firm consists of a set of equations for sales, costs, assets, profits, profit rate, and profit margin that together capture the dynamic relationships among these fundamental business variables. The estimated system of equations is to be used for finding the probable paths of these variables in the future expected to result from today's managerial decisions. This chapter presents a business analysis model of the firm. The first part presents the model and their equations, and the second part reviews the derivation of the model. Our model is based on previous work published in Chap. 2 of Anari and Kolari's *The Power of Profit* (2009). Here, we utilize this model as an analytical tool for conventional firms to conduct simulations of the impact of managerial decisions on sales, costs, assets, profits, profit rate, and profit margin.

2.1 Business Model

FIRM is a program designed to be used for conventional, unregulated-profit firms. Table 2.1 shows model *FIRM* consisting of three equations to be estimated using logarithms (log) of sales (s), capital stocks (k), and profit rate (r). One lag of these variables (i.e., the value of the variable in the previous period) is used in the

A. Anari and J.W. Kolari, *Excel-Based Business Analysis: Forecasting Key Business Trends*, SpringerBriefs in Business 8, DOI 10.1007/978-1-4614-2050-7_2,
© Ali Anari and James W. Kolari 2012

Table 2.1 Business analysis model *FIRM* for simulation

	Initial conditions	s_t, r_t, m_t, k_t
(**2.1.1**)	Sales model	$s_{t+1} = \beta_0 + \beta_1 r_t + \beta_2 m_t + \beta_3 k_t$
(**2.1.2**)	Capital stocks model	$k_{t+1} = \alpha_0 + \alpha_1 s_t + \alpha_2 r_t + \alpha_3 m_t$
(**2.1.3**)	Profit rate model	$r_{t+1} = \theta_0 + \theta_1 s_t + \theta_2 m_t + \theta_3 k_t$
(**2.1.4**)	Profit margin model	$m_{t+1} = r_{t+1} + k_{t+1} - s_{t+1}$
		$S_t = antilog(s_t)$, $K_t =$ antilog (k_t), $R_t =$ antilog (r_t),
		and $M_t =$ antilog (m_t)
(2.1.5)	Total profit model	$Z_{t+1} = S_{t+1} \times M_{t+1}$
(2.1.6)	Total cost model	$C_{t+1} = S_{t+1} - Z_{t+1}$

Bold numbered equations are empirically estimated by regression analyses, and other equations are derived from their forecasts. All equations are solved simultaneously or recursively in forecasting and simulation analyses
The variables are defined as follows: $S(s) =$ sales in current dollars (log), $K(s) =$ capital stocks in current dollars (log), $R(r) =$ profit rate (log), $M(m) =$ profit margin (log), $Z =$ profit in current dollars, and $C =$ total costs in current dollars

equations for projections of the variables. Projections of log profit margin (m), total profits (Z), and total costs (C) are then estimated using forecasts of sales, capital stocks, and profit rate generated from the estimated three equations. Equation (2.1.1) uses values of capital stocks (k_t), profit rate (r_t), and profit margin (m_t) in period t for forecasting log of sales (s_{t+1}) in period $t+1$. In (2.1.2), logs of sales (s_t), profit rate (r_t) and profit margin (m_t) in period t are used for forecasting log of capital stocks (k_{t+1}) in period $t+1$. Equation (2.1.3) employs logs of capital stocks (k_t), sales (s_t), and profit margin (m_t) in period t for forecasting profit rate (r_{t+1}) in period $t+1$. In (2.1.4), the forecast of log of profit margin (m_{t+1}) in period $t+1$ is obtained using forecasts of logs of sales (s_{t+1}), capital stocks (k_{t+1}), and profit rate (r_{t+1}) in period $t+1$. Taking antilogs of the logs of sales (s_{t+1}), capital stocks (k_{t+1}), profit rate (r_{t+1}), and profit margin (m_{t+1}) gives the values of these variables, or S_{t+1}, K_{t+1}, R_{t+1}, and M_{t+1}, respectively. Equation (2.1.5) forecasts total profits (Z_{t+1}) in period $t+1$ as the product of profit margin (M_{t+1}) and sales (S_{t+1}) in period $t+1$. And, (2.1.6) forecasts total costs (C_{t+1}) in period $t+1$ as the difference between sales (S_{t+1}) and total profits (Z_{t+1}) in period $t+1$.

As will be shown in the next chapter, the program *FIRM* has an Excel worksheet for simulation of the impact of changes in total costs, total sales, and total assets on the expected future values of these variables in addition to the future values of total profit, profit rate, and profit margin.

2.2   Derivation of the Model

The business analysis model *FIRM* presented in Sect. 2.1 is derived from a model of the firm proposed in Chap. 2 of Anari and Kolari's *The Power of Profit* (2009). These authors used two approaches, mathematical economics and accounting definitions, for deriving the model. This section presents (1) the foundations of the model based on accounting definitions and (2) its system equations approach. Chap. 3 provides step-by-step applications of the models.

2.2.1   Foundations of the Model FIRM

The average profit rate R_t in period t commonly calculated by firms is defined as the dollar value of nominal profit or earnings Z_t in period t generated from capital stocks divided by the total market value of the capital stocks K_t, or

$$R_t = \frac{Z_t}{K_t}. \tag{2.1}$$

Profit margin in period t is defined as nominal profit Z_t divided by the dollar value of nominal output in either sales or value-added terms:

$$M_t = \frac{Z_t}{S_t}. \tag{2.2}$$

Solving for Z_t in (2.1) and (2.2), we alternatively obtain

$$Z_t = R_t K_t = M_t S_t. \tag{2.3}$$

No matter how profit is defined (before or after charging interest costs, taxes, depreciation, etc.), the identities (2.1) and (2.2) result in (2.3) as long as the same figure for profit is used for computing R_t and M_t. Solving for K_t, S_t, R_t, and M_t results in the following equations:
Capital stocks equation:

$$K_t = \frac{S_t M_t}{R_t}, \tag{2.4}$$

Sales or output equation:

$$S_t = \frac{R_t K_t}{M_t}, \tag{2.5}$$

Profit rate equation:

$$R_t = \frac{S_t M_t}{K_t}, \tag{2.6}$$

Profit margin equation:

$$M_t = \frac{R_t K_t}{S_t}. \tag{2.7}$$

Equation (2.4) is a valuation model of capital stocks. In this equation the value of the stock of capital is the discounted value or capitalized value of profit, in which the numerator shows profit as the product of sales and the profit margin, and the denominator is the discount rate equal to the average profit rate.

Equation (2.5) can be viewed as a sales or production behavior model of managers in the business sector. Consider a firm that has capital stocks K. The firm's capital stocks comprise the bundle of investment goods selected by the firm in the past based on expected hurdle profit rates. The firm's management is expected to attain the profit rate R used for selecting investment projects, which means that R is the target profit rate. Multiplying the expected target profit rate by the amount of capital stocks gives the expected target total profit, or $Z_t = R_t K_t$. In order to attain the expected target profit, the firm must achieve a target level of sales or output derived by multiplying the expected target profit $(Z_t = R_t K_t)$ and expected sales to profit ratio $\left(\frac{1}{M_t} = \frac{Y_t}{Z_t}\right)$ to get $S_t = \frac{R_t K_t}{M_t}$, viz., (2.5). While ex-post realized profit rates and profit margins can be negative on a firm basis or even on an industry basis, *expected* target profit rates and profit margins are positive, due to the fact that firms do not embark on production activities unless they anticipate positive profits in the future.

Equation (2.6) shows that profit rate (R_t) can be computed using K_t, S_t and M_t, and (2.7) shows that profit margin (M_t) can be computed using K_t, S_t, and R_t.

Note that (2.3)–(2.7) are all in terms of profit measures. Equations (2.3), (2.6), and (2.7) are total profit, profit rate, and profit margin, respectively. In the capital stocks equation (2.4), the numerator is total profit, and the denominator is profit rate. In the production equation (2.5), the numerator is total profit, and the denominator is profit margin.

2.2.2 A System Equation Approach

Market participants know the concepts of profit rate and profit margin and intuitively understand the relationships among the values of sales, capital stocks, total profit, profit rate, and profit margin as shown in (2.1)–(2.7). Interconnections between these business variables are informally used by firms and market participants for forecasting, capital budgeting, profit planning, investment analysis, etc. In Anari and Kolari (2009), these relationships are formally developed as a model of the firm to be estimated and used for the same purposes. Here we present a simpler version of the model of the firm presented there.

The dependency of the fundamental business variables on one another shown above means that in the real world the magnitudes of these variables are determined simultaneously. For this reason, systems of dynamic equations containing five equations for the five variables (i.e., sales, capital stocks, total profit, profit rate, and profit margin) are the most appropriate and potentially useful empirical representation of the model.

As an initial step to developing the model for a firm, we take the logarithms of both sides of capital stocks equation (2.4), sales equation (2.5), profit rate equation (2.6), and profit margin equation (2.7) resulting in the following simple contemporaneous relationships (i.e., relationships in the same period) between the logarithms of S_t, K_t, R_t, and M_t:

$$k_t = s_t + m_t - r_t, \tag{2.8}$$

$$s_t = r_t + k_t - m_t, \tag{2.9}$$

$$r_t = s_t + m_t - k_t, \tag{2.10}$$

$$m_t = r_t + k_t - s_t, \tag{2.11}$$

where the coefficients of the principle variables in the model (s_t, r_t, m_t, and k_t) are either plus or minus one as posited by theory, and there is no residual error.

Next, it is reasonable to assume that firms and market participants use lagged values of the profit rate, profit margin, capital stocks, and sales to form conditional expectations or forecasts of their current and future values. The simplest approach to modeling expectations when forecasting each variable in period $t+1$ is to use the values of other variables in the previous period t as follows:

$$k_{t+1} = \alpha_0 + \alpha_1 s_t + \alpha_2 r_t + \alpha_3 m_t, \tag{2.12}$$

$$s_{t+1} = \beta_0 + \beta_1 r_t + \beta_2 m_t + \beta_3 k_t, \tag{2.13}$$

$$r_{t+1} = \theta_0 + \theta_1 s_t + \theta_2 m_t + \theta_3 k_t, \tag{2.14}$$

$$m_{t+1} = \eta_0 + \eta_1 r_t + \eta_2 k_t + \eta_3 s_t, \tag{2.15}$$

where the left-hand-side variables are expected values or forecasts of capital stocks, sales, profit rate, and profit margin, respectively, for period $t+1$ using the values of the other variables in the previous period t. A constant term is added to each equation for econometric estimation of the equations. Note that when lags of the variables are used for forming expectations, the coefficients on the lagged variables are no longer equal to plus or minus unity and residual error exists. To minimize residual errors in these equations, other variables can be included in the set of variables used for forecasting the fundamental business variables.

Equations (2.12)–(2.15) can provide estimates of expectations or forecasts of capital stocks, sales, profit rate, and profit margin. Different econometric methods can be applied for their estimation. When using a system approach for estimating all the equations, we can reduce the number of equations (and hence coefficients) to be estimated by using the forecasts of the variables generated in the model. For instance, (2.15) can be derived from estimates of (2.12)–(2.14). Table 2.1 provides a model of a conventional firm dubbed *FIRM* comprised of dynamic relationships among sales, capital stocks, profit rate, profit margin, and total profit represented by equations for these variables. This model can be extended to include more lags of the variables in equations for sales, capital stocks, and profit rate as discussed in Chap. 2 of Anari and Kolari (2009). There the extended model with several lags was augmented to include other variables such as the Federal funds rate and growth rate of debt outstanding, as these variables were found to have significant impacts on the fundamental business variables (sales, capital stocks, profit, profit rate, and profit margin). Due to limitations of Excel for handling large models (i.e., models with many lags and variables), we specified only one lag of the variables in the model.

Chapter 3
Applications of Business Analysis Model *FIRM*

Abstract This chapter provides step-by-step instructions for applying the business model *FIRM* to Home Depot Company using time series of sales, total costs, and total assets for this company. The chapter covers the data used; estimated equations for sales, assets, and profit rate; and forecasts of fundamental business variables, including sales, total costs, total assets, total profits, profit rate, and profit margin. The estimated models are also used for simulations of cost reduction, sales projections, and investment evaluation. Following these steps, managers can readily apply *FIRM* to their own firm.

Keywords Estimated equations • Business forecasts • Business simulation • Cost reduction • Sales projections • Investment evaluation

In this chapter, we show how to use the Excel-based profit system model *FIRM* to do a business analysis of Home Depot, a nationwide home improvement company found in most US cities. We use the model to forecast trends in their key business variables, such as sales, total costs, assets, total profits, profit rate, and profit margin. Also, the program allows the simulation of the probable outcomes of alternative managerial decisions, including cost reduction, investment strategies, and sales projections.

We use annual data series for sales, total costs, and capital stocks from Home Depot's annual financial statements. We opted to employ annual data because they contain more long-run information and are less volatile than quarterly data.

The total cost time series selected is the sum of costs of goods sold and selling plus general and administrative expenses. For capital stocks, we use two measures: (1) the sum of property, plant, and equipment values (PPENT), and (2) total assets. Data for sales, total costs, and capital stocks should be in the same dollar units— that is, thousand dollars, million dollars, and so forth. As will be shown in this chapter, choices with respect to sample periods, capital stocks, and total costs result in different estimated equations for sales, capital stocks, and profit rate and, in turn, lead to different generated simulation results. In practice, the users should rely on their own judgment in choosing data and sample periods.

A. Anari and J.W. Kolari, *Excel-Based Business Analysis: Forecasting Key
Business Trends*, SpringerBriefs in Business 8, DOI 10.1007/978-1-4614-2050-7_3,
© Ali Anari and James W. Kolari 2012

While the model presented in Chap. 2 requires capital stocks in market values, firm data for Home Depot measure capital stocks in terms of historical book values. Consequently, our forecasts will not be accurate. For instance, it is possible that an initial increase in capital stocks may result in a lower level of capital stocks in the next period due to the fact that book values rather than market values are used.

3.1 Applications of the Model to Home Depot

We illustrate the application of the profit system model *FIRM* for business analyses of Home Depot by showing the Excel worksheets on the computer screen generated in the application process. The application begins by downloading *FIRM* and saving it as *FIRM_HomeDepot.xlsm*. It is important to use file type Excel Macro-Enabled (*xlsm*) for saving the file so that the software can use the program written in Microsoft Visual Basic. We assume that the user has installed Analysis Toolpak VBA and that the Excel sheet displays "Developer" (see Preface).

3.1.1 Getting Data into FIRM_HomeDepot.xlsm Excel File

The first step in time series analysis is to read your data into the Excel file named *FIRM_HomeDepot.xlsm*. Figure 3.1 shows an Excel file containing a data table to be used as input data for Home Depot. The dataset consists of annual time series of

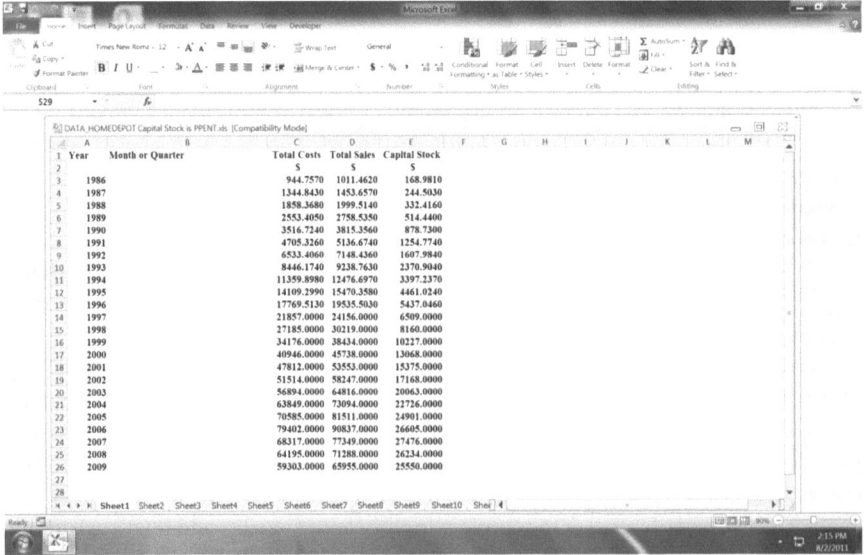

Fig. 3.1 Input data for FIRM_HomeDepot.xlsm Model, capital stocks measured as PPENT, variables are in $Million

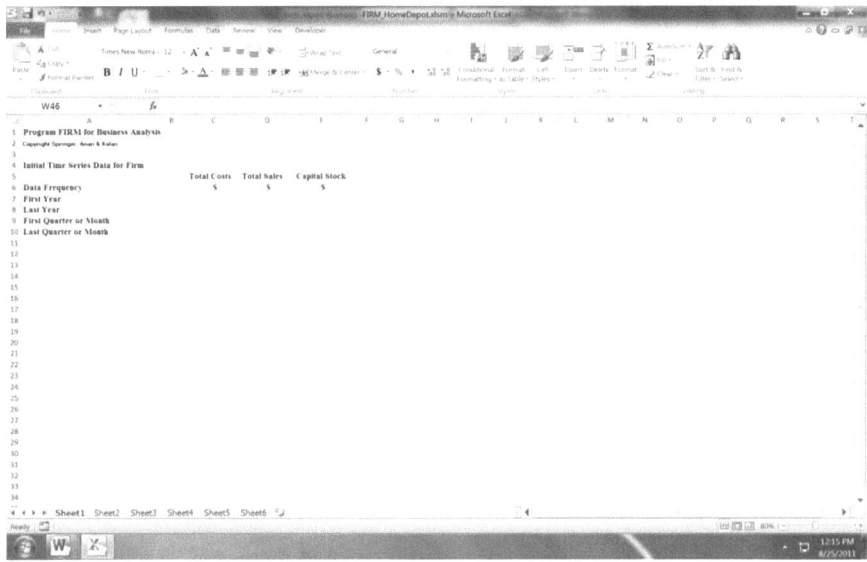

Fig. 3.2   Sheet1 of FIRM_HomeDepot.xlsm Model before data entry

total costs, total sales, and capital stocks from 1986 to 2009 in millions of dollars. Capital stocks equal the sum of property, plant, and equipment in historical book values.

Figure 3.2 shows Sheet1 of *FIRM_HomeDepot.xlsm* before data entry. Before the *FIRM* program can read in the data, we need to tell program *FIRM* a little about the time series data—that is, data frequency, when it begins and when it ends. Cells B6–B10 are used to enter information about the time series. The user needs to enter "a" or "q" or "m," all in lower cases, in cell B6 for annual, quarterly, and monthly data, respectively. If other keys are entered, then an error message is prompted. Since our data here are annual, we insert "a" in Cell B6 and press Enter. The first year of the data should be inserted in cell B7. We enter 1986, the first year of our data series, in cell B7. The last year of the data should be inserted in cell B8. We enter 2009, the last year of our data series, in cell B8. If the data series are quarterly or monthly, then the first quarter or month should be entered in cell B9. For instance, if the quarterly data runs from the second quarter of 1986, then we enter 2 in cell B9. The last quarter or month should be entered in cell B10. For instance, if the quarterly data ends in the third quarter of 2009, then we enter 3 in cell B10.

The data for cells B7–B10 are numeric and integer. If non-numeric or non-integer data are entered, then an error message is prompted. Also, the software checks whether the data are valid. The first and last quarters are from 1 to 4, and the first and last months are from 1 to 12.

The next step is to enter time series data. Using Copy and Paste commands, we copy the data and paste them into Sheet1 of *FIRM_HomeDepot.xlsm* as shown in

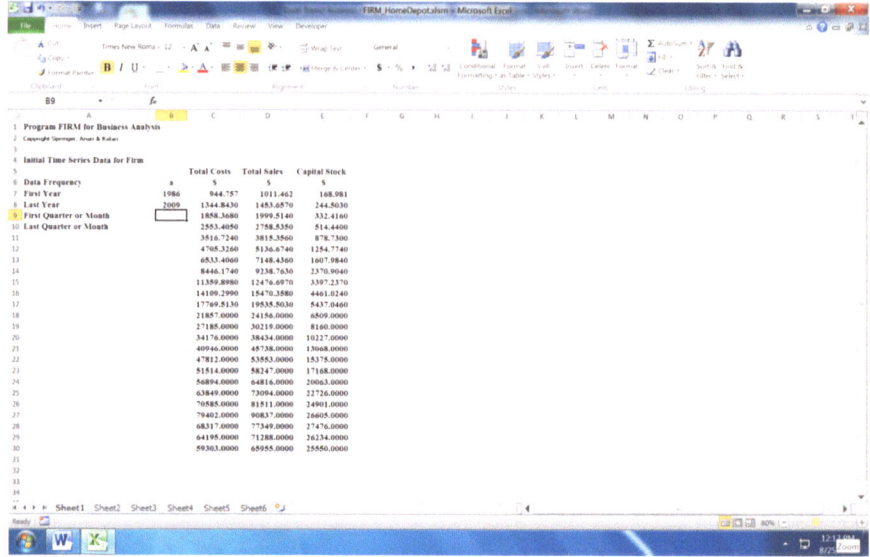

Fig. 3.3 Sheet1 of FIRM_HomeDepot.xlsm Model after data entry

Fig. 3.3. The time series of total costs should be entered in column C beginning with cell C7—that is, cell C7 contains the first observation for total costs. The time series of total sales should be entered in column D beginning with cell D7—in other words, cell D7 contains the first observation for total sales. The time series of total capital stocks should be entered in column E beginning with cell E7—as such, cell E7 contains the first observation for capital stocks.

The minimum number of observations for estimating the model is 13. If the number of observations is less than 13, then the program prompts an error message.

3.1.2   Analysis Using the Sum of Property, Plant, and Equipment Values for Capital Stocks

Now click on "Developer" and then click on "Macro." You will see Fig. 3.4 on the screen. Click on Run. The program responds by showing Fig. 3.5 on the screen asking "Do You Want To Perform Simulations?" Select No. This option should be selected when the program is run for the first time because the program does not yet have initial values for simulations. After you have clicked Run, the software generates spreadsheets 2–6. Click on Sheet2 at the bottom of the Excel sheet and you see Sheet2, Time Series of Fundamental Variables in the Model shown in Fig. 3.6. In column B of this worksheet, you see the "Year" column generated by the software beginning 1986 in cell B7. Using the data in cells B6–B10 of Sheet1,

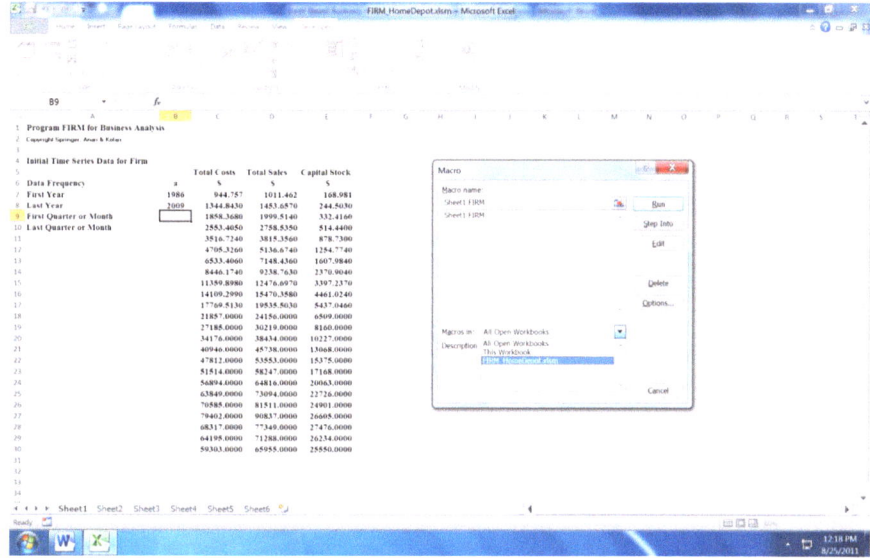

Fig. 3.4 Click Developer, Click on Macro, Click on Run

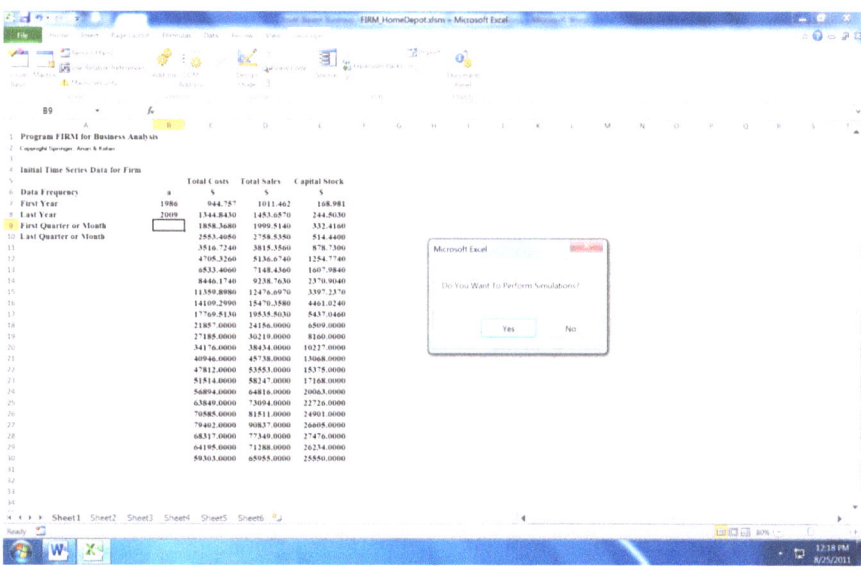

Fig. 3.5 Click on No

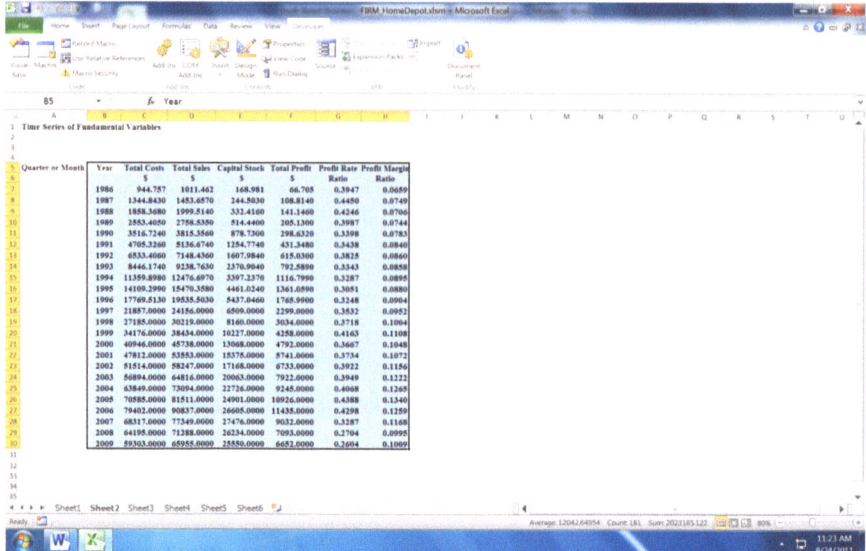

Fig. 3.6 Sheet2 of FIRM_HomeDepot.xlsm Model, time series variables are *highlighted*

the software generates the data table shown in Fig. 3.6. Time series data in columns C, D, and E in Sheet2 are the same as columns C, D, and E in Sheet1 containing time series of total costs, total sales, and capital stocks. Column F of Sheet2 contains total profit time series computed as the difference between total sales in column D and total costs in column C of Sheet2. Deducting the time series of total costs from the sales time series gives time series of earnings or profits. Column G of Sheet2 contains the profit rate time series computed as the ratio of profit in column F to capital stocks in column E. Column H of Sheet2 contains profit margin time series computed as the ratio of profit in column F to sales in column D.

The estimated equations for sales, capital stocks, and profit rate are presented in Sheet3 as shown in Figs. 3.7–3.9. For each equation, Excel Sheet3 shows the estimated coefficients of the variables, their standard deviations, *t*-values, *R*-squared values, adjusted *R*-squared values, sum of squared residuals in the equations, standard errors of regressions, means of the dependent variables, standard deviations of the dependent variables, Durbin–Watson statistics, and *F* statistics. These statistical outputs provide the users with a knowledge of regression analysis information to decide whether the model can be accepted for forecasting and simulation purposes.

Next, clicking on Sheet4 gives projections of the variables and their initial values from 2010 to 2014 as shown in Fig. 3.10. The initial conditions for costs, sales, capital stocks, profits, profit rate, and profit margin are the values of these variables in the last year of the time series, in this case in 2009. When annual data are used, the model generates forecasts of the variable for a 5-year time

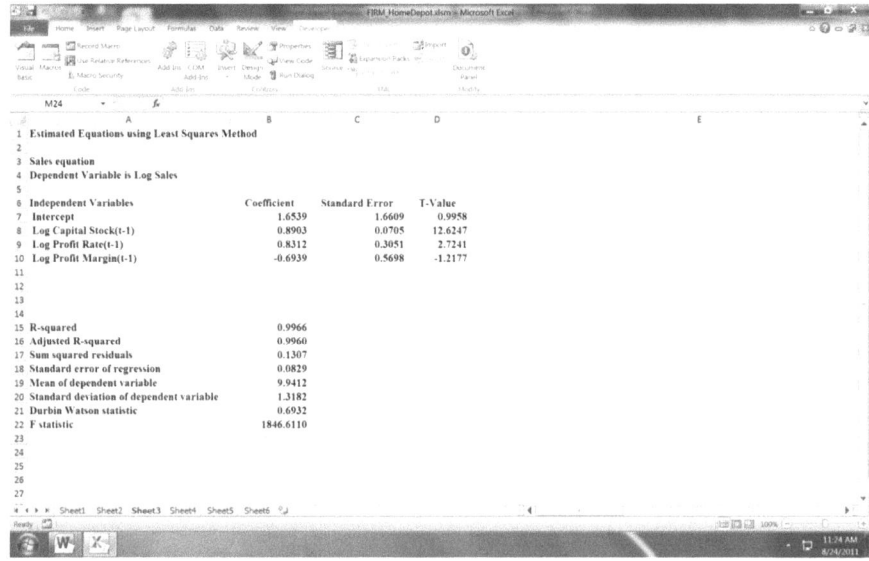

Fig. 3.7   Sheet3 of FIRM_HomeDepot.xlsm Model, Columns A–D, estimated sales equation

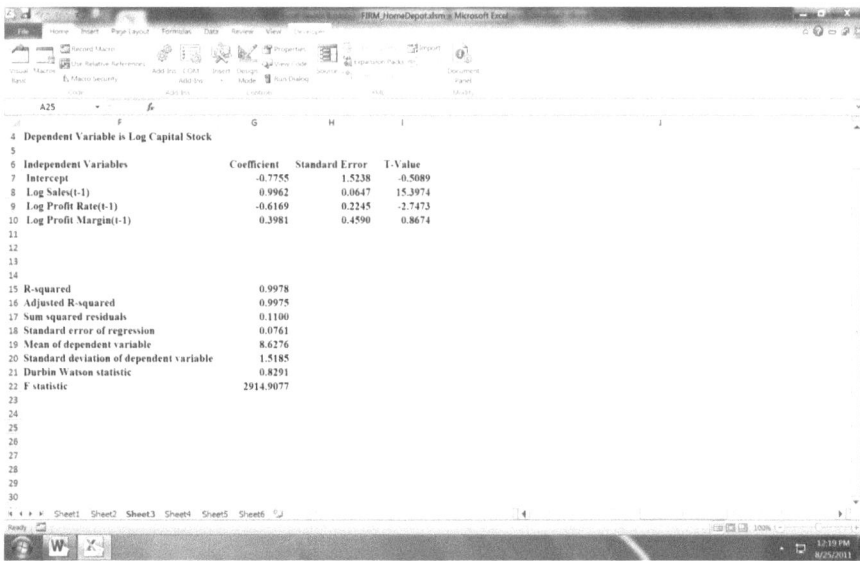

Fig. 3.8   Sheet3 of FIRM_HomeDepot.xlsm Model, Columns F–I, estimated capital stocks equation

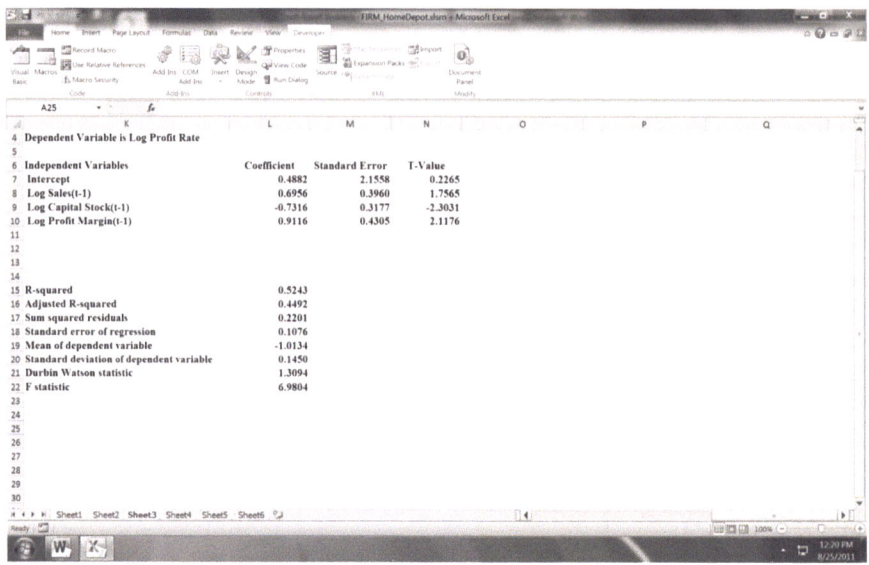

Fig. 3.9 Sheet3 of FIRM_HomeDepot.xlsm Model, Columns K–N, estimated profit rate equation

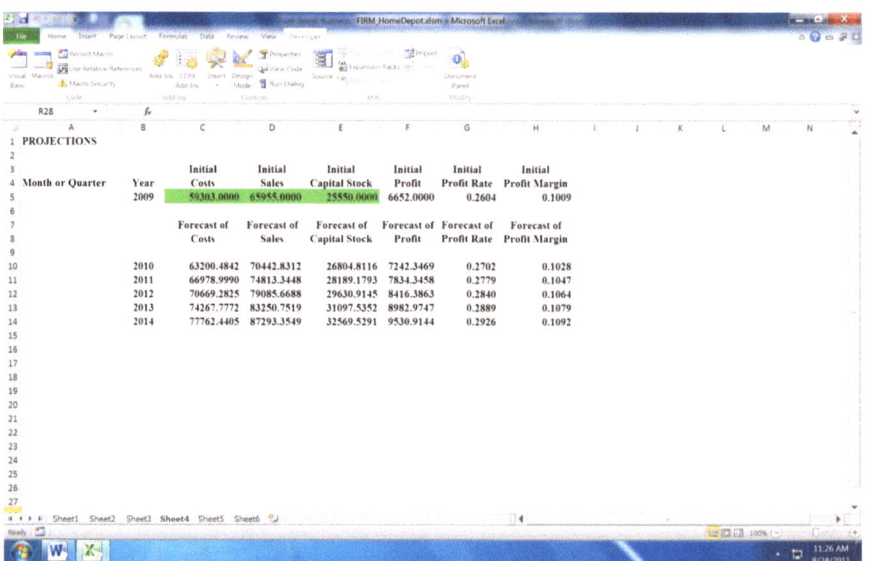

Fig. 3.10 Sheet4 of FIRM_HomeDepot.xlsm Model, projections

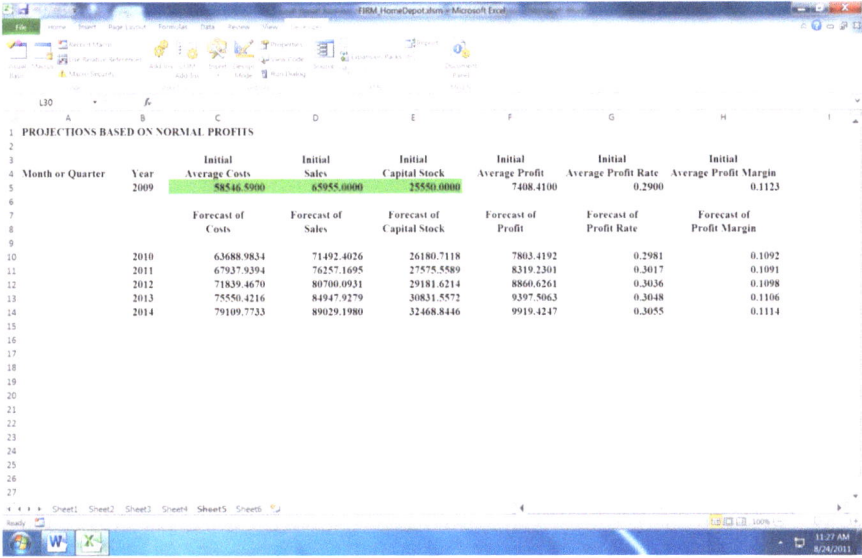

Fig. 3.11 Sheet5 of FIRM_HomeDepot.xlsm Model, projections based on normal profits

horizon. For quarterly and monthly data, the model generates a 20-quarter forecast horizon and a 60-month forecast horizon, respectively.

Clicking on Sheet5 gives projections based on normal profits in the last period—that is, 2009 (Fig. 3.11). The magnitudes of the business variables (sales, capital stocks, and profit rate) in the last period play a key role in forecasting, as the model uses business data in 2009 for the initial conditions to generate forecasts. Abnormal profits in the last period may underestimate or overestimate forecasts of the variables in the forecast horizon. For this reason, the model computes normal profits in the last period, computes profit rate and profit margin based on normal profits, and uses the normalized data for forecasting. The computations are done in the following steps: (1) the sum of total costs and total sales for all periods (in this case from 1986 to 2009) is computed, (2) total costs are deducted from total sales to obtain total profits from 1986 to 2009, (3) total profits are divided by total sales for computing normal profit margin, (4) sales in the last period is multiplied by the normal profit margin to compute normal profit in the last period, and (5) normal profit is divided by capital stocks in the last period to get normal profit rate.

Clicking on Sheet6 gives a worksheet for simulation shown in Fig. 3.12. The framework of the simulation worksheet in Sheet6 is similar to Sheet4 and Sheet5 with cells C5, D5, and E5 highlighted in green for the initial values of costs, sales, and capital stocks. To begin the simulation, we go to Sheet4 and Copy cells C5, D5, and E5 and Paste on cells C5, D5, and E5 in Sheet6, as shown in Fig. 3.13. If in this stage we rerun the model by clicking on Developer, clicking on Macro, and responding "Yes" to "Do You Want to Perform Simulations?" shown in Fig. 3.14, then Sheet6 gives initial values and forecasts for the variables shown in Fig. 3.15,

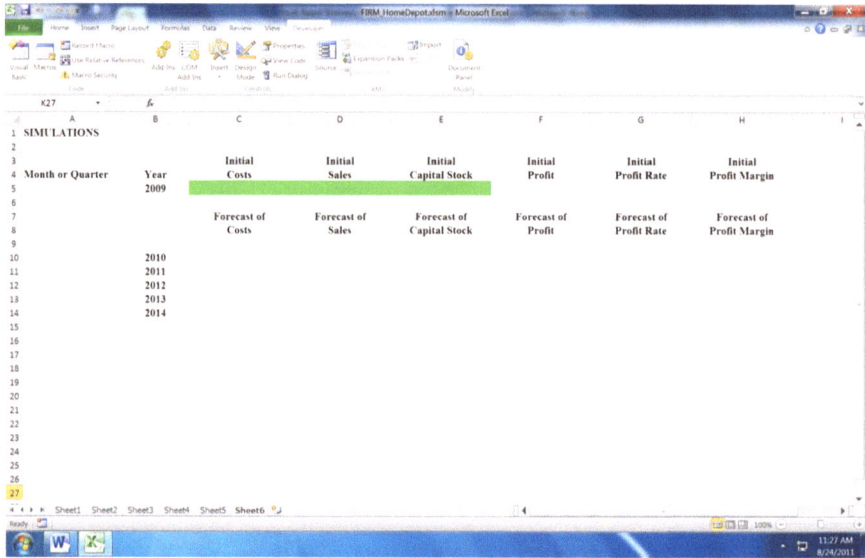

Fig. 3.12 Sheet6 of FIRM_HomeDepot.xlsm Model, simulation worksheet

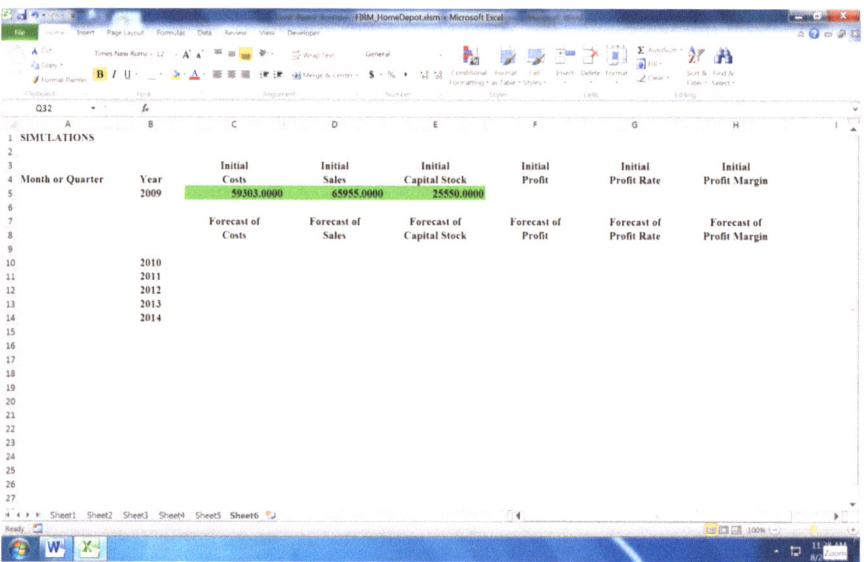

Fig. 3.13 Sheet6 of FIRM_HomeDepot.xlsm Model, simulation worksheet, pasting initial conditions

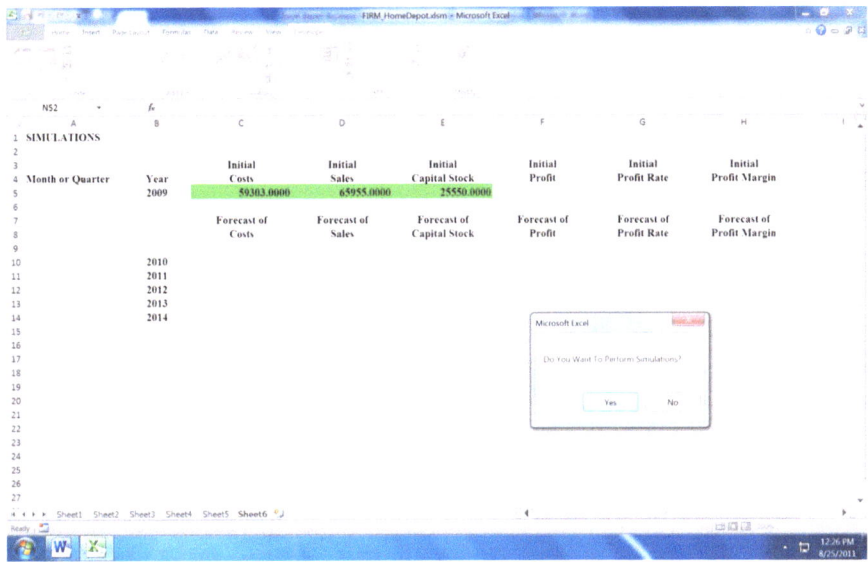

Fig. 3.14 FIRM_HomeDepot.xlsm Model, simulation question

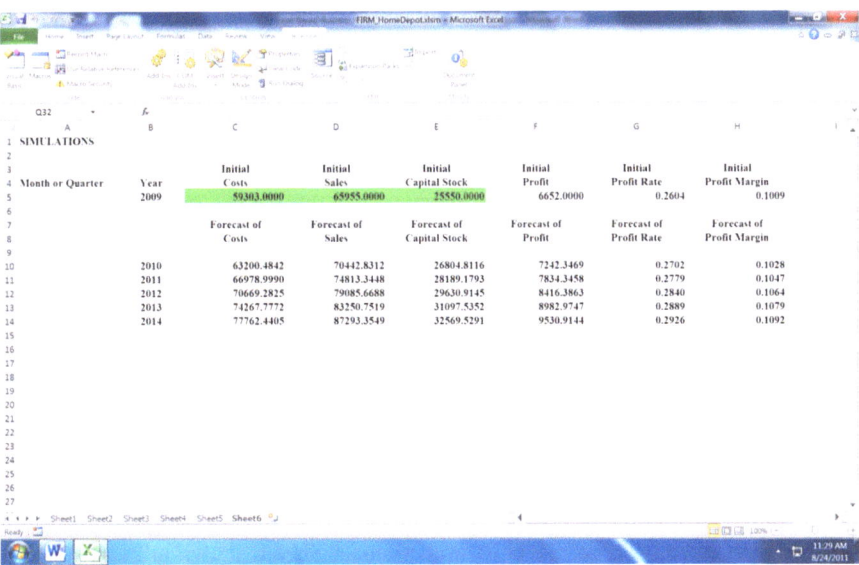

Fig. 3.15 Sheet6 of FIRM_HomeDepot.xlsm Model, simulation results with initial conditions unchanged

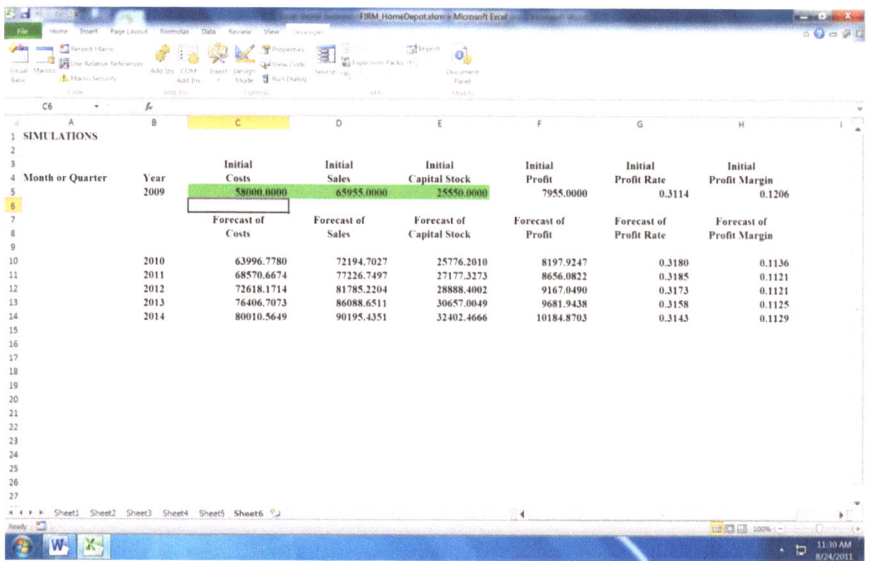

Fig. 3.16 Sheet6 of FIRM_HomeDepot.xlsm Model, simulation results for cost reduction

which are the same as those shown in Sheet4 shown in Fig. 3.10. The program reads cells C5–E5 from Sheet6; computes profit, profit rate, and profit margin; inserts them in cells F5–H5 in Sheet6; uses values of the variables in line 5 as the initial conditions for forecasting; and then computes forecasts for the period from 2010 to 2014 shown in Sheet6. Alternatively, we can use initial values of costs, sales, and capital stocks from cells C5, D5, and E5 in Sheet5 for initial values.

Simulations of the impact of managerial decisions on costs, sales, and capital stocks are performed by changing the initial values of costs, sales, and capital stocks in cells C5, D5, and E5 in Sheet6, and then rerunning the model for generating new forecasts of these variables and forecasts of total profit, profit rate, and profit margin. To simulate the impact of a cost reduction decision, we enter 58,000 in cell C5 in Sheet6, rerun the model by clicking Developer, then click Macro, and then respond "Yes" to the question "Do You Want to Perform Simulations?" Figure 3.16 shows the simulation results for reducing the total costs of operations from the initial $59,303 million to $58,000. Compared to the initial case in Sheet4, profit in 2010 is projected to increase from $7,242.3 to $8,197.9, profit rate from 0.270 to 0.318, and profit margin from 0.102 to 0.113.

Suppose that the cost reduction is attained by a capital stocks investment of $450 million so that the new initial capital stocks are expected to be $26,000 million. By entering 26,000 in cell E5 and pressing Enter, clicking on Developer > Macro, and responding "Yes" to the "Do You Want to Perform Simulations?" question prompted on screen, we get the new projections in Sheet6 shown in Fig. 3.17.

Figure 3.18 shows simulation results in Sheet6 for the case when initial sales is expected to increase from $65,955 million to $66,500 million as a result of more investment in capital stocks.

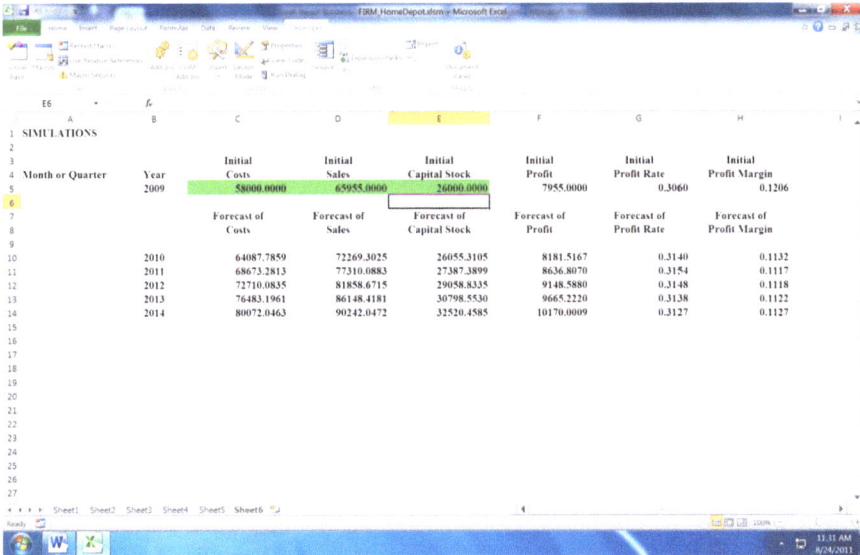

Fig. 3.17 Sheet6 of FIRM_HomeDepot.xlsm Model, simulation results for capital formation

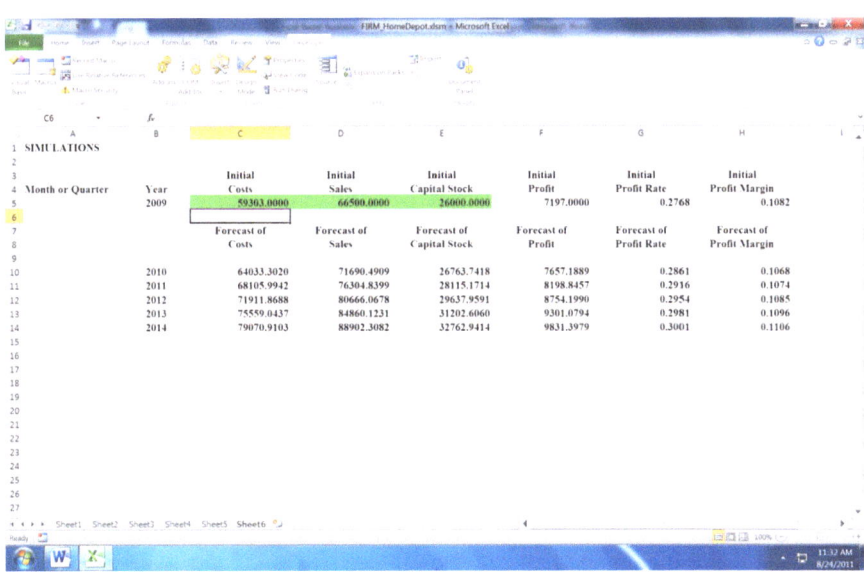

Fig. 3.18 Sheet6 of FIRM_HomeDepot.xlsm Model, simulation results for projected sales

Figure 3.19 shows simulation results in Sheet6 for the case when initial sales is expected to increase from $65,955 million to $66,500 million, but normal costs ($58,546.59 million) are assumed from Sheet5.

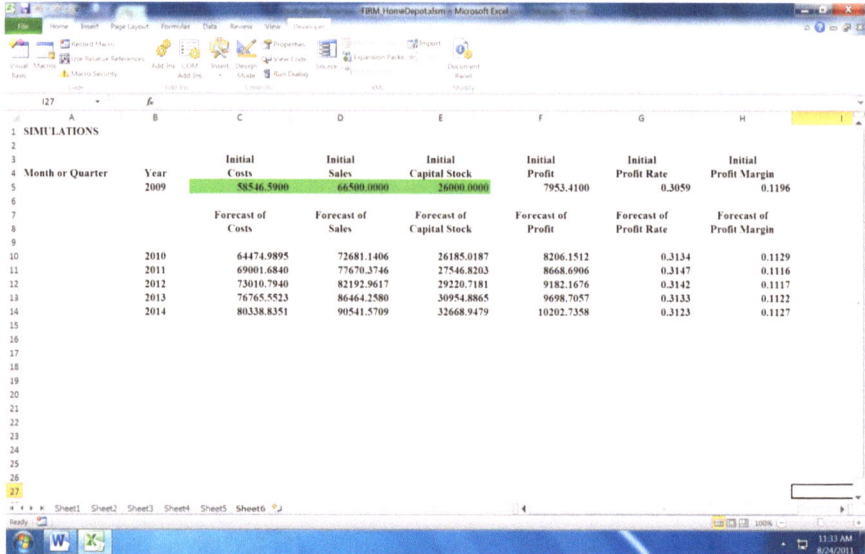

Fig. 3.19 Sheet6 of FIRM_HomeDepot.xlsm Model, simulation results for projected sales and normal costs

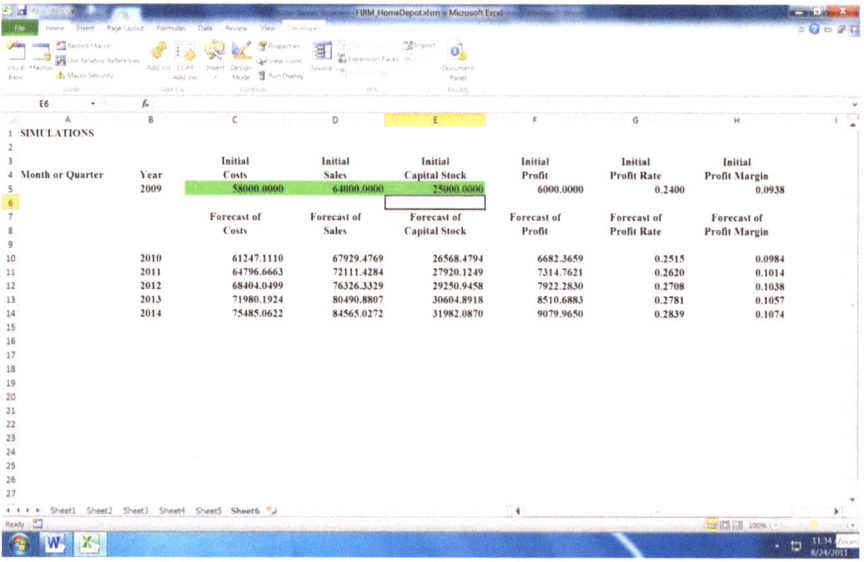

Fig. 3.20 Sheet6 of FIRM_HomeDepot.xlsmModel, simulation results for projected reduced sales and costs

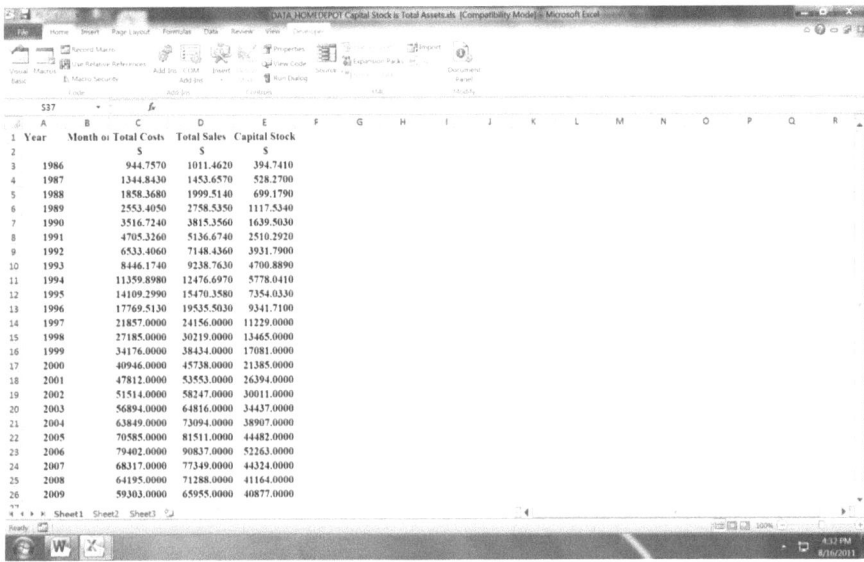

Fig. 3.21 Input data for FIRM_HomeDepot.xlsm Model, capital stocks measured as total assets

Figure 3.20 shows simulation results in Sheet6 for the case when initial sales, initial costs, and initial capital stocks are expected to decrease to $64,000 million, $58,000 million, and $25,000 million, respectively.

3.1.3   Analysis Using Total Assets for Capital Stocks

Figure 3.21 shows initial data for Home Depot when using total assets (i.e., the sum of property, plant, and equipment plus financial assets) for capital stocks. Total costs and sales data are the same as before, only capital stocks data are changed. Again, we copy the initial data and paste the data on columns C–E, beginning with cells C7–D7 of Sheet1 of *FIRM_HomeDepot.xlsm*, as shown in Fig. 3.22. Using total assets for capital stocks also changes the time series of profit rate, given that profit rate is total profits divided by capital stocks. Figure 3.23 shows Sheet2 containing the time series of capital stocks and profit rate when total assets are used for capital stocks. Rerunning the model, Figs. 3.24–3.26 show estimated equations for sales, capital stocks, and profit rate in Sheet3, and Fig. 3.27 shows Sheet4 containing projections generated from the model when these equations are used. Figure 3.28 shows projections based on normal profits in 2009. Figures 3.29 and 3.30 show simulation results for cost reduction and capital formation (Sheet6). Figures 3.31–3.33 show expected sales projections based on different initial conditions.

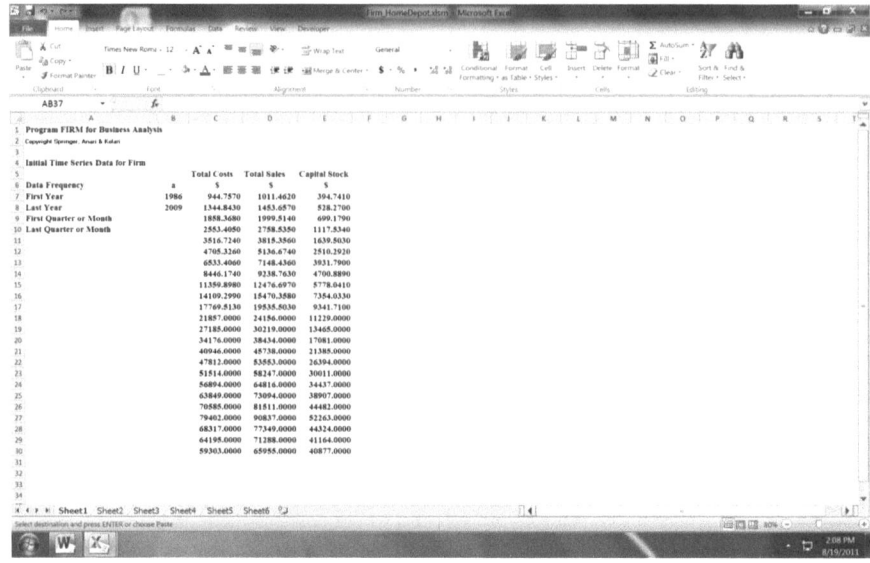

Fig. 3.22 Sheet1 of FIRM_HomeDepot.xlsm Model after data entry

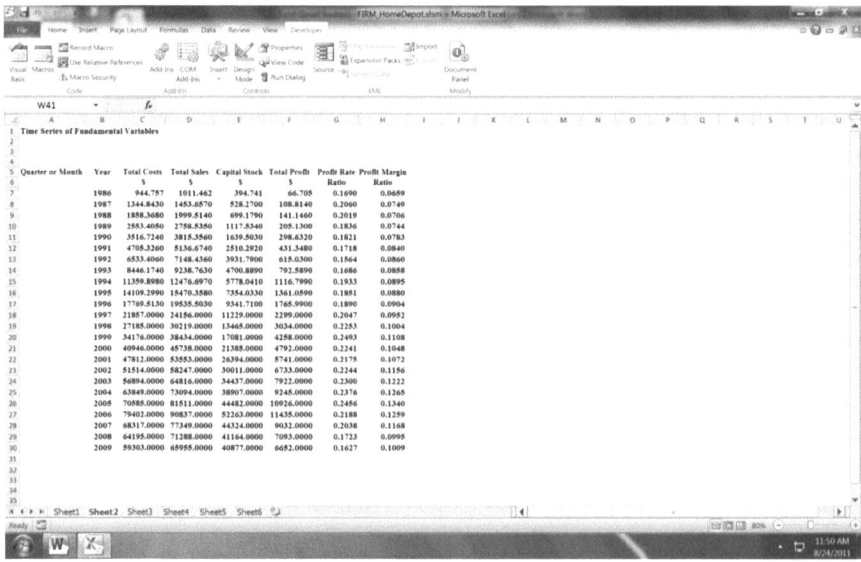

Fig. 3.23 Sheet2 of FIRM_HomeDepot.xlsm Model, time series of variables in the model

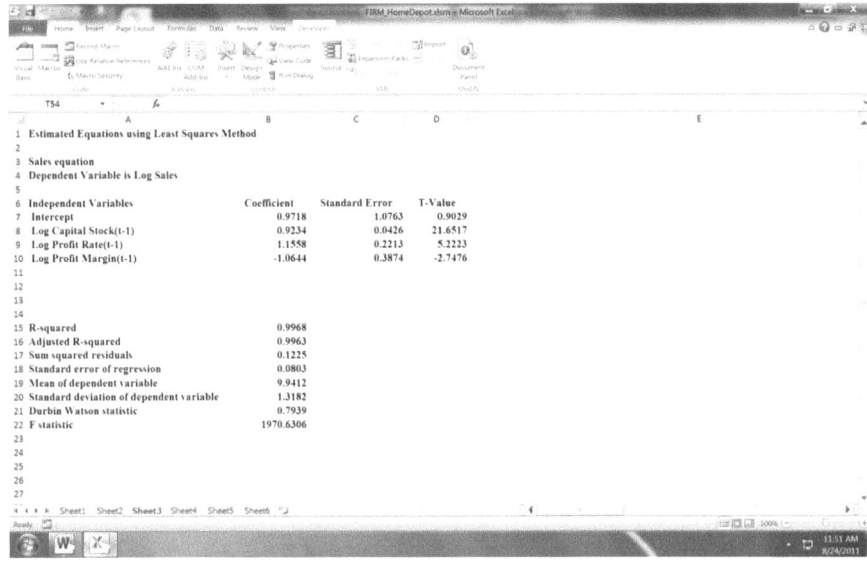

Fig. 3.24 Sheet3 of FIRM_HomeDepot.xlsm Model, Columns A–D, estimated sales equation

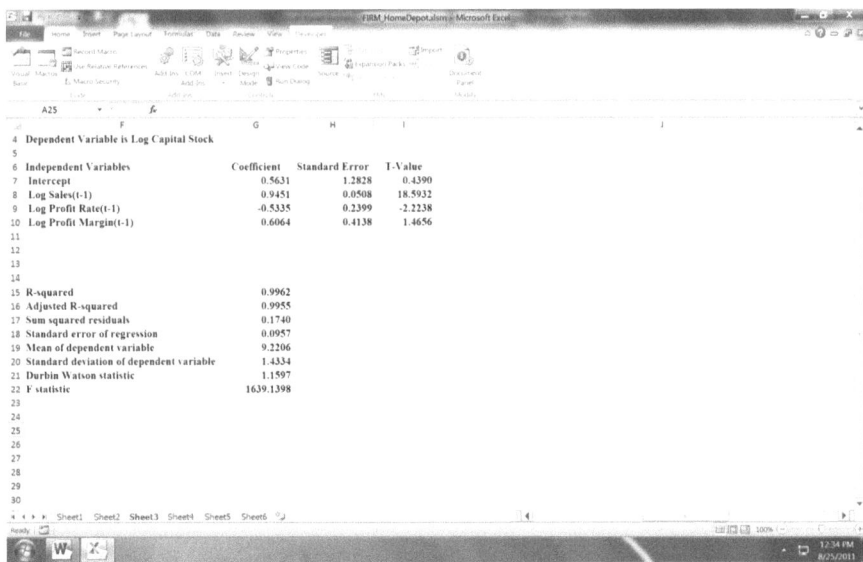

Fig. 3.25 Sheet3 of FIRM_HomeDepot.xlsm Model, Columns F–I, estimated capital stocks equation

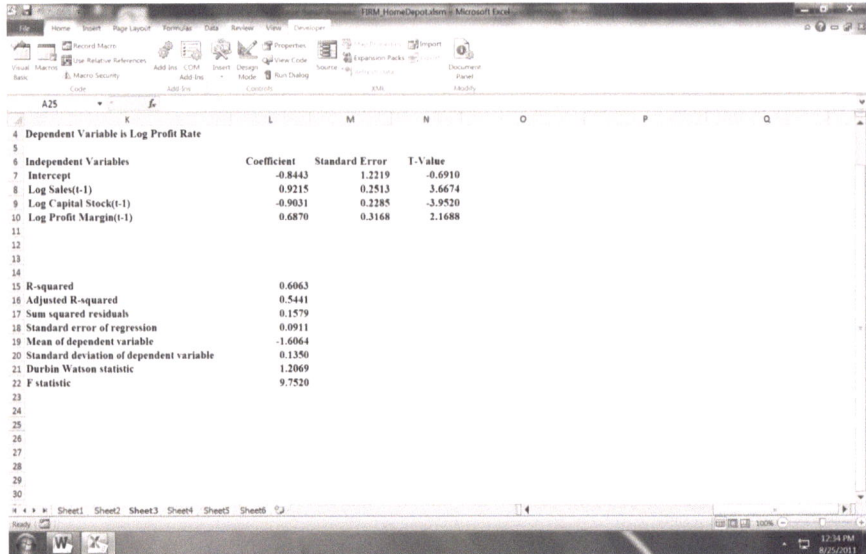

Fig. 3.26 Sheet3 of FIRM_HomeDepot.xlsm Model, Columns K–N, estimated profit rate equation

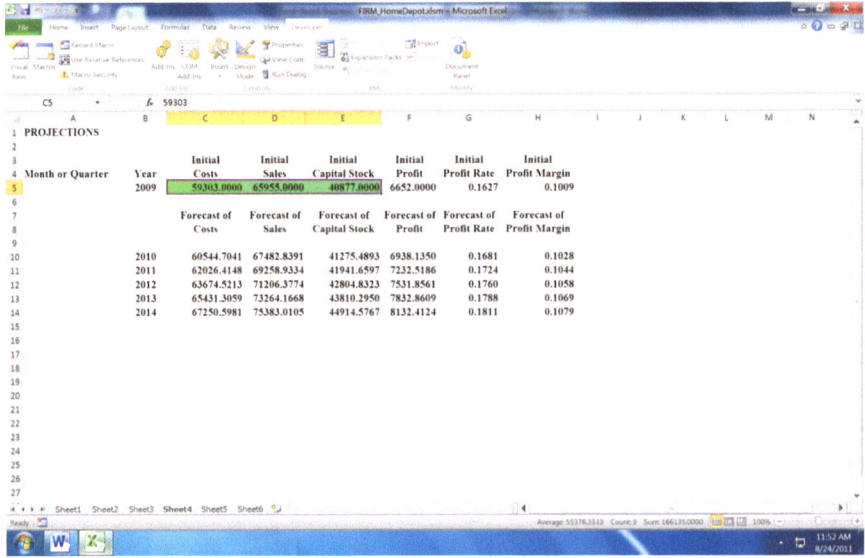

Fig. 3.27 Sheet4 of FIRM_HomeDepot.xlsm Model, projections

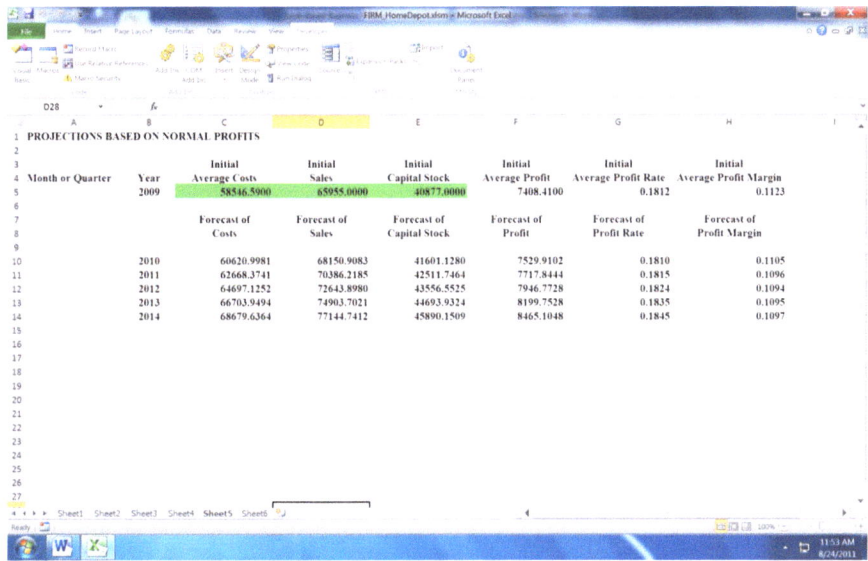

Fig. 3.28 Sheet5 of FIRM_HomeDepot.xlsm Model, projections based on normal profits

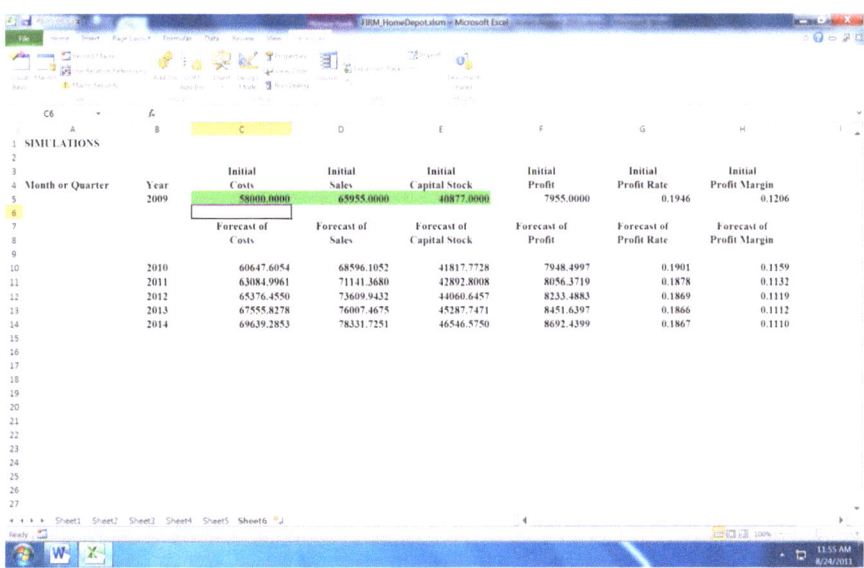

Fig. 3.29 Sheet6 of FIRM_HomeDepot.xlsm Model, simulation results for cost reduction

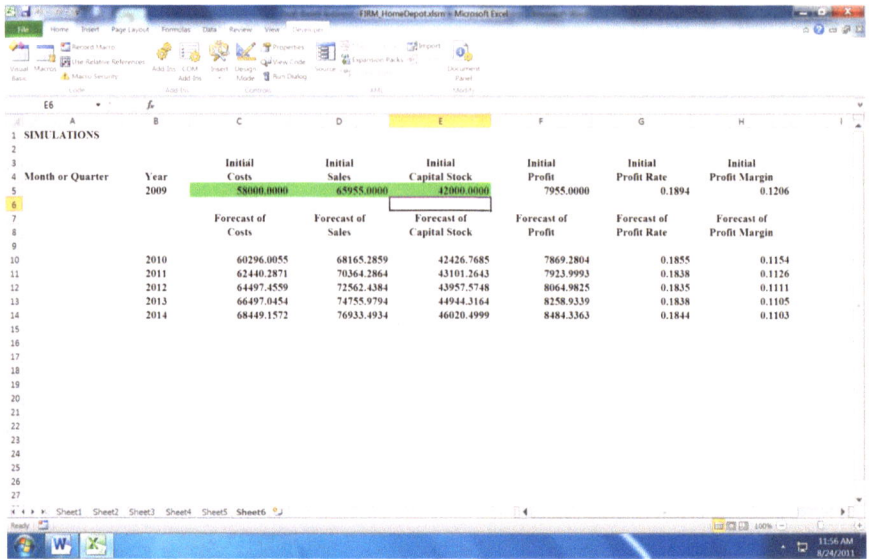

Fig. 3.30 Sheet6 of FIRM_HomeDepot.xlsm Model, simulation results for capital formation

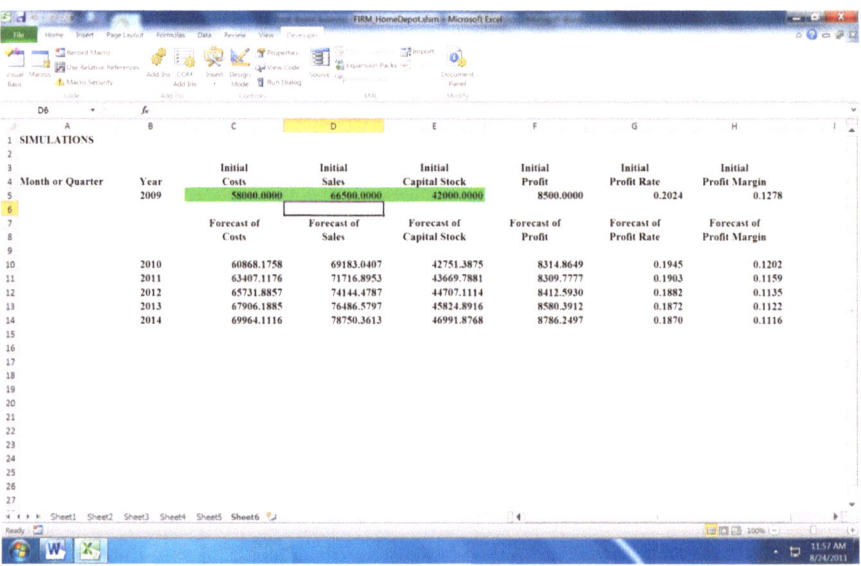

Fig. 3.31 Sheet6 of FIRM_HomeDepot.xlsm, simulation results for projected sales

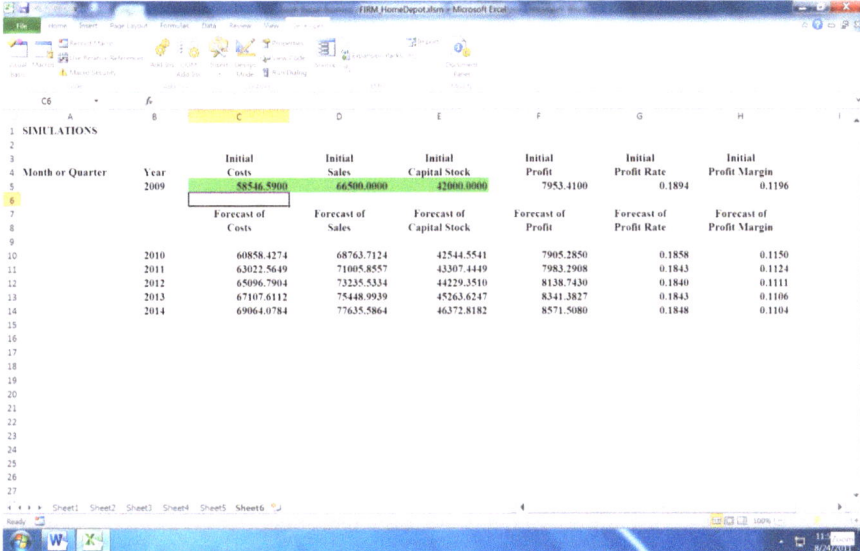

Fig. 3.32 Sheet6 of FIRM_HomeDepot.xlsm, simulation results for projected sales and normal costs

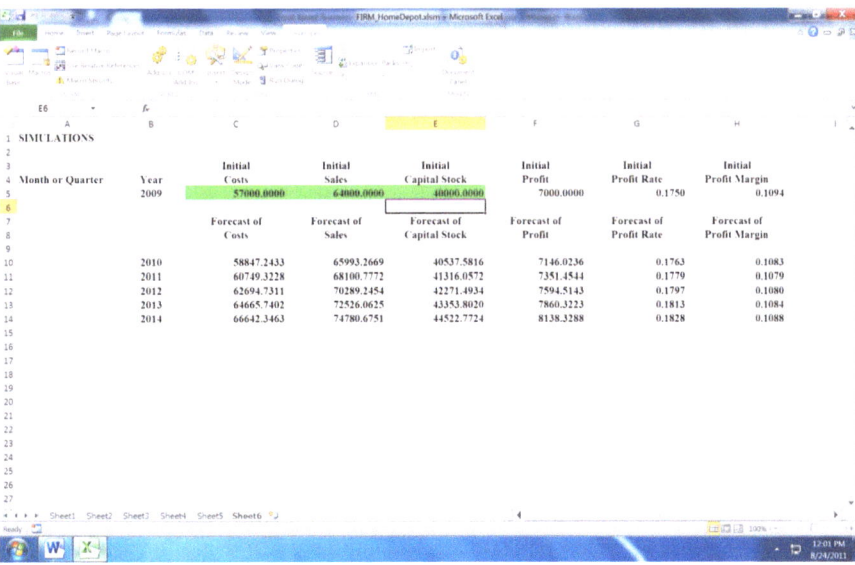

Fig. 3.33 Sheet6 of FIRM_HomeDepot.xlsm Model, simulation results for projected reduced sales and costs

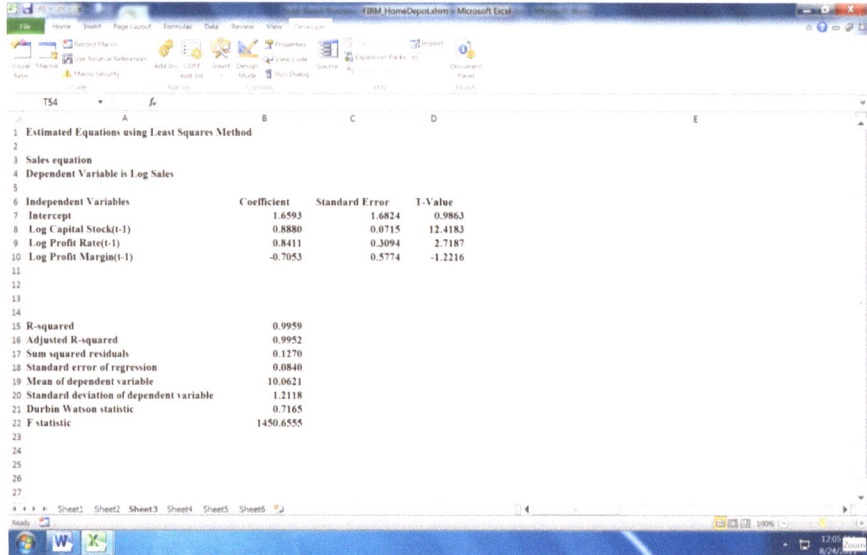

Fig. 3.34 Sheet3 of FIRM_HomeDepot.xlsm Model, Columns A–D, estimated sales equation, capital stocks measured as PPENT, sample period 1987–2009

3.1.4 Changing Sample Periods

The choice of the sample period can have significant impact on the model's projections. Different sample periods result in different estimates of the coefficients of the model in sales, capital stocks, and profit rate equations, and different forecasts of the variables in the model. When the sample size is small, then adding or dropping one observation in the sample can have a significant impact on the estimates of the coefficients of the variables in the model as well as on the forecasts generated from the model. Dropping the 1986 observation from the sample and rerunning the model using annual data from 1987 to 2009 result in new estimates of equations for sales, capital stocks, and profit rate, as shown in Figs. 3.34–3.36 when capital stocks equal the sum of PPENT. Figures 3.37 and 3.38 show new projections based on estimated equations when using the sample from 1987 to 2009. Figures 3.39–3.41 show new estimates of equations for sales, capital stocks, and profit rate when capital stocks are the sum of property, plant, and equipment plus financial assets using the sample period from 1987 to 2009. Figures 3.42 and 3.43 show new projections based on estimated equations when using the sample from 1987 to 2009 and capital stocks as total assets.

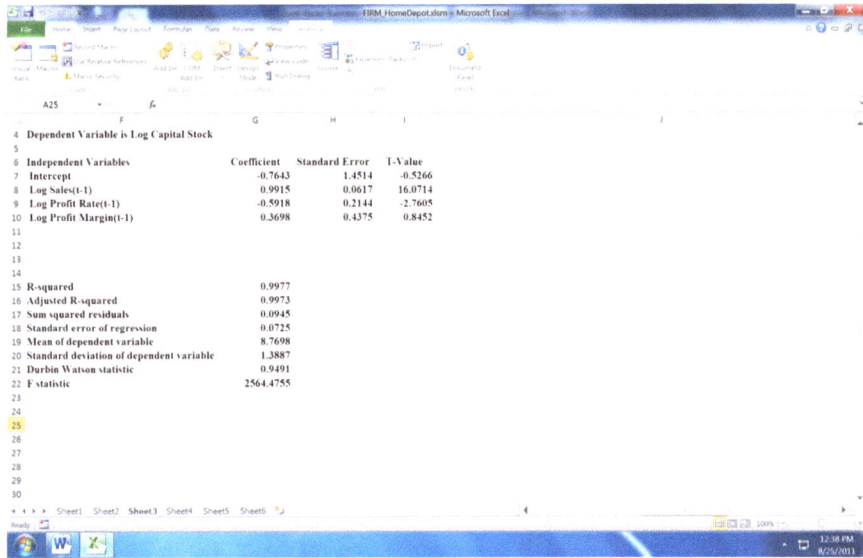

Fig. 3.35 Sheet3 of FIRM_HomeDepot.xlsm Model, Columns F–I, estimated capital stocks equation, capital stocks measured as PPENT, sample period 1987–2009

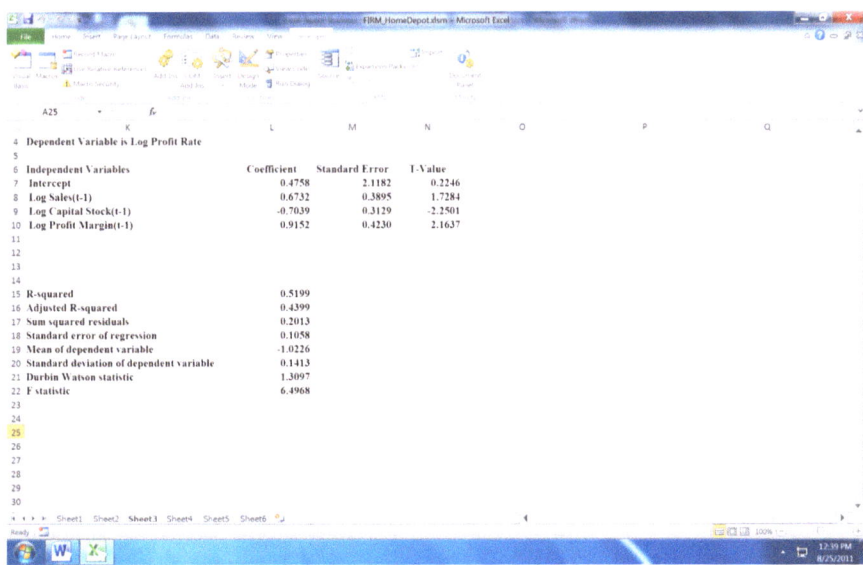

Fig. 3.36 Sheet3 of FIRM_HomeDepot.xlsm Model, Columns K–N, estimated profit rate equation, capital stocks measured as PPENT, sample period 1987–2009

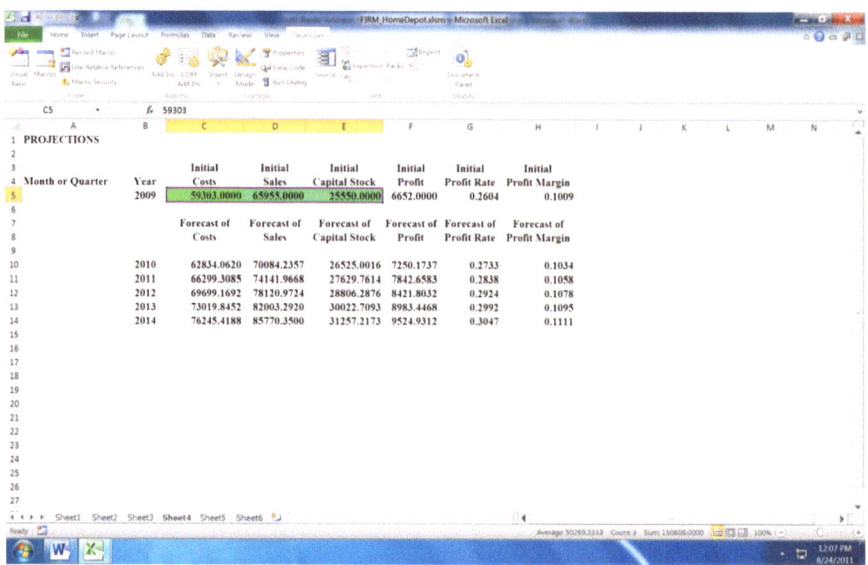

Fig. 3.37 Sheet4 of FIRM_HomeDepot.xlsm Model, projections, capital stocks measured as PPENT, sample period 1987–2009

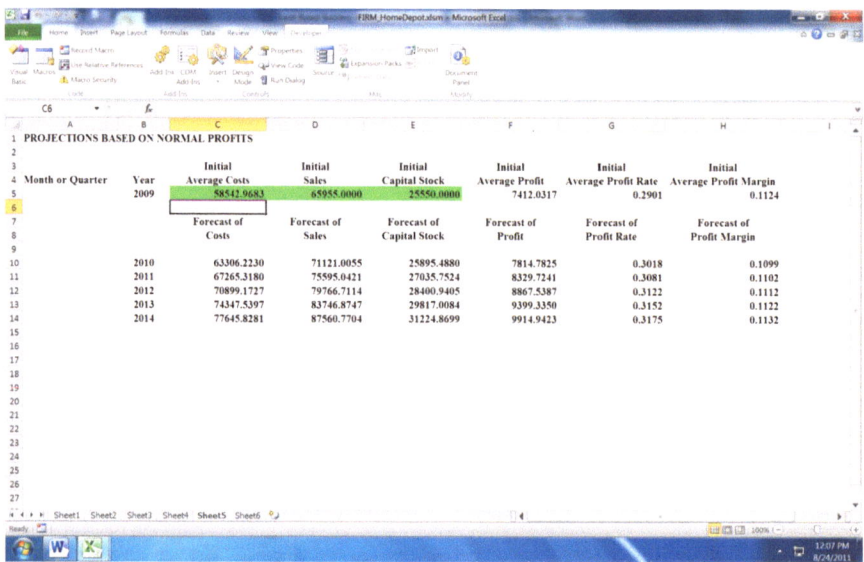

Fig. 3.38 Sheet5 of FIRM_HomeDepot.xlsm Model, projections based on normal profits, capital stocks measured as PPENT, sample period 1987–2009

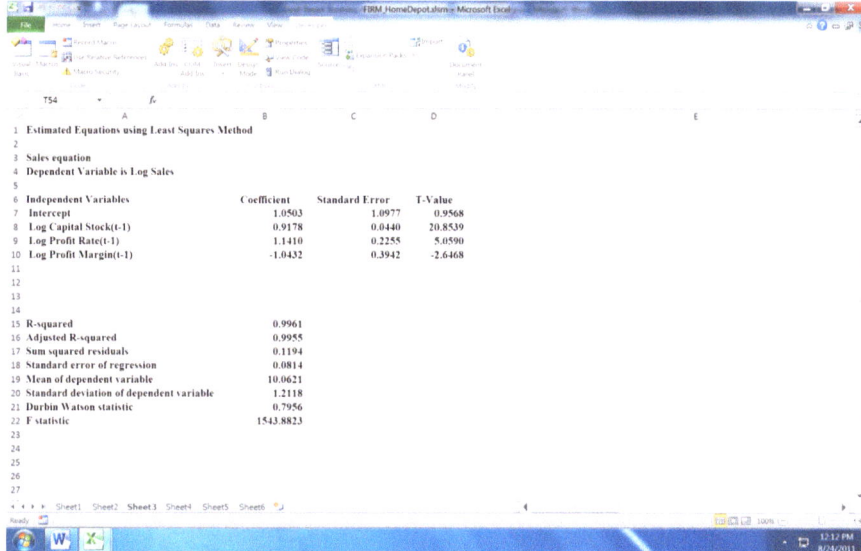

Fig. 3.39 Sheet3 of FIRM_HomeDepot.xlsm Model, Columns A–D, estimated sales equation, capital stocks measured as total assets, sample period 1987–2009

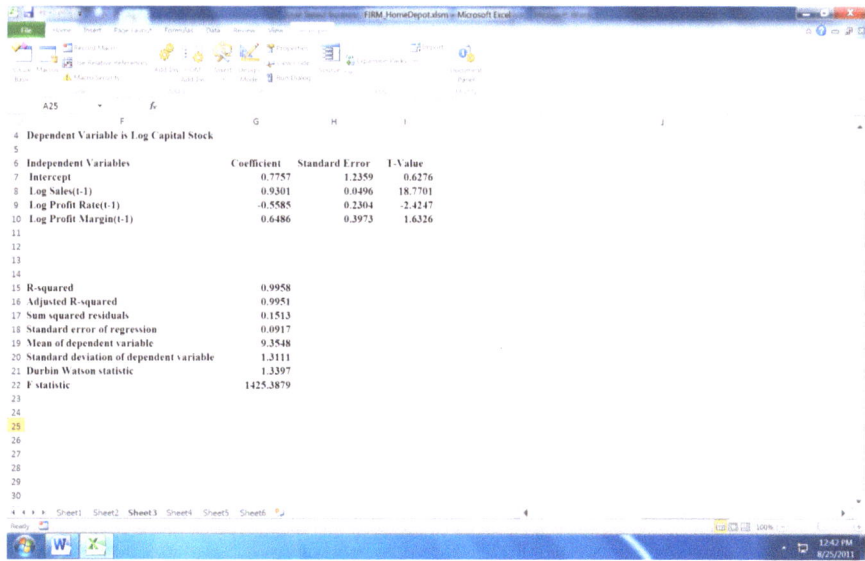

Fig. 3.40 Sheet3 of FIRM_HomeDepot.xlsm Model, Columns F–I, estimated capital stocks equation, capital stocks measured as total assets, sample period 1987–2009

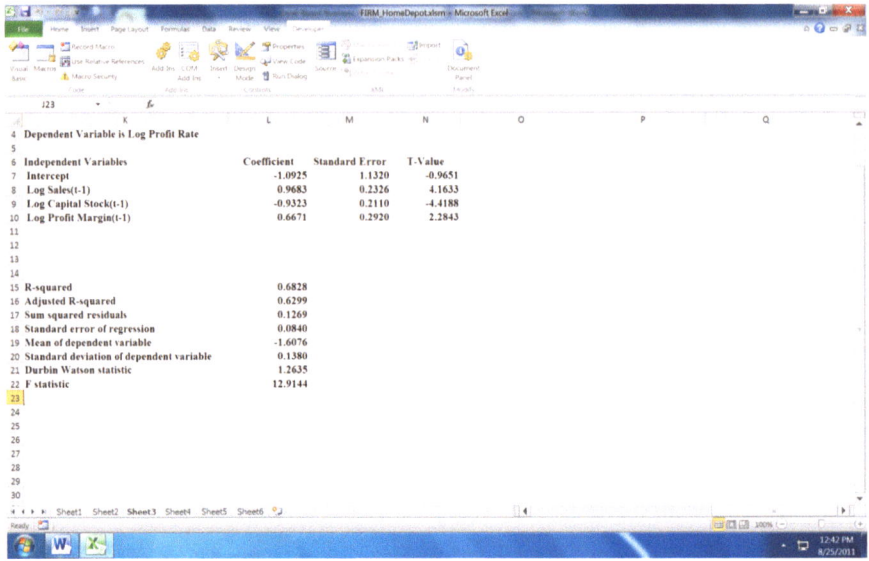

Fig. 3.41 Sheet3 of FIRM_HomeDepot.xlsm Model, Columns K–N, estimated profit rate equation, capital stocks measured as total assets, sample period 1987–2009

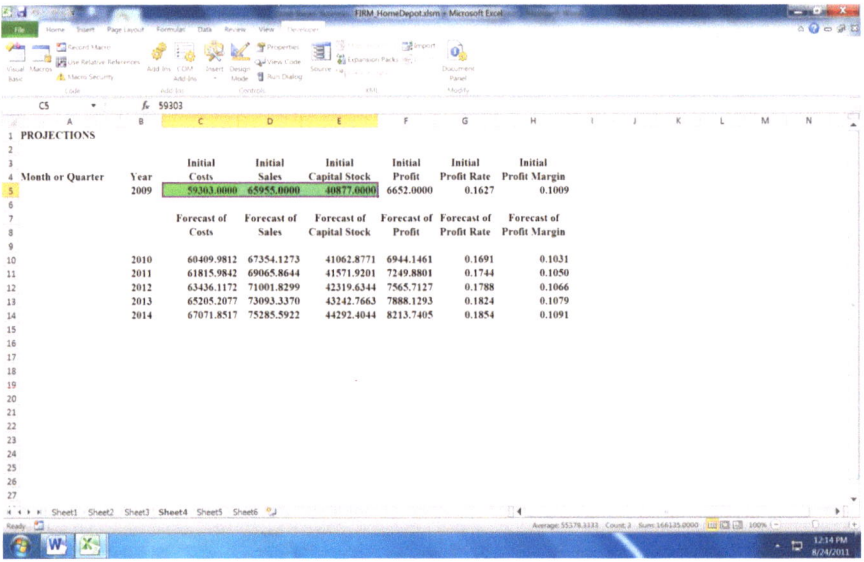

Fig. 3.42 Sheet4 of FIRM_HomeDepot.xlsm Model, projections, capital stocks measured as total assets, sample period 1987–2009

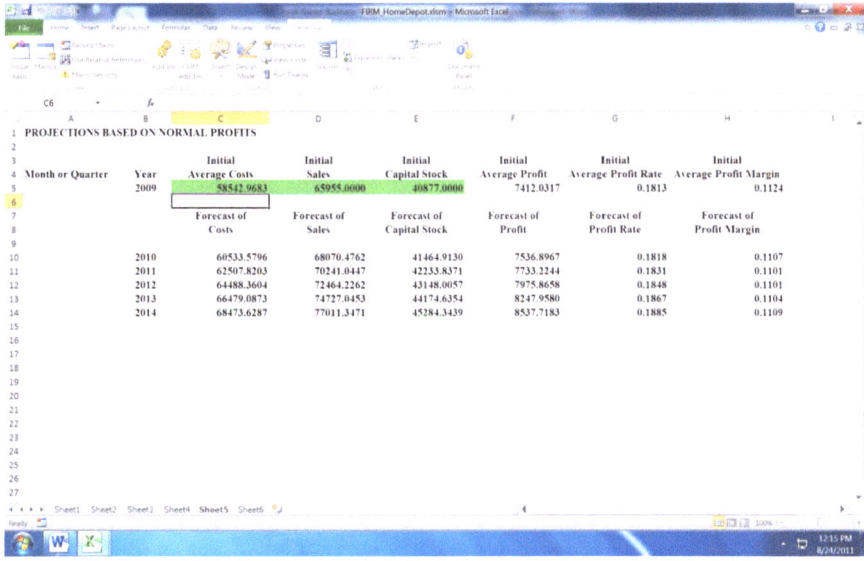

Fig. 3.43 Sheet5 of FIRM_HomeDepot.xlsm Model, projections based on normal profits, capital stocks measured as total assets, sample period 1987–2009

Table 3.1 Comparison of forecasts of sales for home depot in 2010 with actual sales

Sample period	Initial conditions	Capital stocks	Forecast $Million	Actual $Million	Forecast error
1986–2009	As in 2009	PPENT	70,442	67,997	−2,445
1986–2009	Normal profits	PPENT	71,492	67,997	−3,495
1986–2009	As in 2009	Total assets	67,482	67,997	515
1986–2009	Normal profits	Total assets	68,150	67,997	−153
1987–2009	As in 2009	PPENT	70,084	67,997	−2,087
1987–2009	Normal profits	PPENT	71,121	67,997	−3,124
1987–2009	As in 2009	Total assets	67,354	67,997	643
1987–2009	*Normal profits*	*Total assets*	*68,070*	*67,997*	*−73*

3.2   Forecast Comparisons

The model results for sales show that the trend in forecast sales is upward. Since we have data for 2010, we can compare actual sales in 2010 and the sales forecast generated by the model with different data used for capital stocks and different sample periods. As Table 3.1 shows, *FIRM* with total assets used for capital stocks and assuming normal profit in 2009 generated the most accurate forecasts compared with forecasts generated by other datasets. Over time, comparisons of actual outcomes with forecasts from different data series provide useful information about which datasets should be used to generate more accurate forecasts.

At the time of writing this book, the U.S. economy was recovering from the Great Recession of 2008–2009. Caution is recommended in using our model in this period due to volatile data series that make economic and financial forecasting difficult.

Chapter 4
Troubleshooting

Abstract This chapter discusses a number of problems the user of the business model *FIRM* may encounter in applications of data for firms, and how to handle these problems.

Keywords Variables and data sources • Negative realized profits • Smoothing data • Initial or base year data • Editing excel sheets

Applications of economic and financial models to real-world problems often face common problems associated with data inputs. While the models may be expressed in neat mathematical relationships, the data for their applications can be messy or entirely unsuitable. Here, we discuss issues related to data sources, the choice of data to measure variables in the model, negative realized profits, smoothing data, and initial data. We also discuss editing excel sheets, using trends, and provide a list of error messages.

4.1 Variables and Data Sources

When applied to an individual firm, the model *FIRM* requires time series of sales, total costs, and capital stocks expressed in terms of their market values.

Annual statements (income statements and balance sheets) for individual firms are the sources of data on revenues (sales), costs, and capital stocks for use in the model. Nowadays, the Internet has become an important source of such data, as many firms post their previous annual statements there. For instance, annual data for Home Depot used in Chap. 3 can be found on the company's Webpage.

In the USA, there are several organizations that provide Web-based business data and research services for a fee, such as Wharton Research Data Services (WRDS). The Compustat North America database contained in WRDS offers annual data from 1950 and quarterly data from 1975Q4 on fundamental business variables. Table 4.1 shows a partial list of variables in the income statement and balance sheet of firms available from WRDS.

A. Anari and J.W. Kolari, *Excel-Based Business Analysis: Forecasting Key Business Trends*, SpringerBriefs in Business 8, DOI 10.1007/978-1-4614-2050-7_4,
© Ali Anari and James W. Kolari 2012

Table 4.1 Variables in income statements and balance sheets

Income statement variables

  Sales (SALE)

  Cost of goods sold (COGS)

  Selling, general, and administration expenses (XSGA)

  Operating income before depreciation (OIBDP)

  Operating income after depreciation (OIADP)

  Interest and related expense (XINT)

  Non-operating income (expense)—total (NOPI)

  Special items (SPI)

  Pretax income (PI)

  Income taxes—total (TXT)

  Income before extraordinary items (IB)

Balance sheet variables

  Assets—total (TA)

  Cash and short-term investments (CHE)

  Receivables—total (RECT)

  Inventories—total (INVT)

  Current assets—other (ACO)

  Current assets—total (ACT)

  Property, plant, & equipment-total(Net) (PPENT)

  Accumulated depreciation, depletion, and amortization (DPACT)

  Investment and advances—equity (IVAEQ)

  Investment and advances—other (IVAO)

  Intangible assets—total (INTAN)

  Assets—other—total (AO)

Source: Wharton Research Data Services (WRDS)

4.2 Choice of Data to Measure Variables

A number of potential problems can arise in the measurement of variables. For example, sales (revenues) may have the problem of non-operating incomes (NOPI) in one or more periods—that is, sales of some items that are not part of the normal business of a firm. If this is the case, then the extraordinary revenues should be excluded from total sales to obtain normal sales. This adjustment is especially important if sales in the last period include revenues from extraordinary items, as the last period sales are used as initial conditions for forecasting.

For the total cost time series, we have the problem of inclusion of extraordinary items, interest charges, depreciation, and taxes. These items can vary considerably from one period to another and can distort the financial performance and business results from normal operations—in particular, the trends in the time series of total costs, total profits, profit rate, and profit margin. For comparisons of the performance of firms or industries, financial analysts use different measures of profits, such as earnings before interest, taxes, depreciation, and amortization (EBITDA), earnings before interest, tax, amortization, and exceptional items (EBITAE), and income before extraordinary items (IB). Depending on the choice of items to be included in total costs, different measures of total profits are computed resulting in different measures of profit rates and profit margins. Whatever measure of total costs are employed, the selected measures can have important impacts on the estimated equations in model *FIRM* presented in Chap. 3, as well as forecasts and simulation analyses. In Chap. 3, we measured the total cost as the sum of costs of goods sold plus selling, general, and administrative expenses. Thus, the profit figures were EBITDA.

For estimating the time series of capital stocks, we encounter two problems: (1) items to be included in the time series of capital stocks and (2) the market value of capital stocks. Panel B of Table 4.1 shows two measures of capital stocks, including a narrow measure where capital stocks are assumed to be comprised of property, plant, and equipment (PPENT), and a broader measure of capital stocks in terms of total assets. In between these two measures of capital stocks, there are several possible measures depending on what balance sheet items are included in the definition of capital stocks.

The second major problem in compiling time series of capital stocks is the lack of market value data. Accounting information on the physical capital stocks of firms is normally in historical book value terms, while the capital stocks in our models are in market value terms. Historical book values contain less information on the productivity of capital stocks and exclude the impact of inflation on their nominal values. The gap between market and book values of capital stocks is important bearing in mind that it is comprised of real estate properties, equipment, software, and inventory. For example, when the values of real estate properties are expressed in book values, they can be substantially lower than their market values due to inflation and other market factors.

Measuring the value of capital stocks for sole proprietorships, partnerships, and the self-employed poses some conceptual problems. There are firms whose main capital stocks are human capital. Consider a firm of accountants that rents its office, equipment, and software. If the firm has no debt outstanding, what is the value of capital stocks for this firm? Of course, it is the market value of the firm if sold to a potential buyer. Some firms, such as a dental practice, own some parts of their capital and rent some parts. Again, the purchase price of this firm is the capital stocks we should use.

Difficulties in measuring capital stocks can affect profit rates in model *FIRM*. Profit rates are defined as profits divided by capital stocks.

In view of these data availability issues, we should note that capital stocks are measured in book value terms in Chap. 3. As the empirical results showed, the estimated equations for profit rates did not have high R^2 values reflecting weaker goodness-of-fit compared with R^2 values for sales and capital stocks. Also, the forecasts of capital stocks may decrease despite increases in capital stocks or profits in initial periods, as forecasts of capital stocks are in book values rather than market values. Most firms know the approximate market values of their capital stocks and can compile time series of capital stocks in market values to be used in model *FIRM*.

4.3 Negative Realized Profits

Another problem in the application of our model to individual firms is the possibility of negative profits, or losses, in some periods. Naturally, expected profits are always positive, as firms do not embark on production or capital formation activities unless they foresee positive expected profits. Losses should not occur in the first place and are unintended consequences of wrong managerial decisions or an incorrect course of managerial actions. If we look at the time series of total costs of firms that have incurred losses in some periods in the past, we see that total costs have been reduced in the aftermath of incurring losses. That is, management has taken corrective actions to reduce total costs to recover profitability. Because revenues are decided by their customers, firms may have little influence over total revenues. By contrast, firms have closer control of their total costs. For this reason, losses in the time series of profit and loss should not be included in the models of firms because they are unintended. In this instance, we recommend that realized losses should be replaced with expected profits.

Since expected profit is always positive, when profit and loss time series include losses in a period, the model *FIRM* assumes a notional small expected profit equal to 0.001% of sales (i.e., total costs are assumed to be reduced). An alternative is to compute a moving average profit time series based on the notion that firm owners and investors normally form their profit expectations based on moving averages of profits in several periods. However, there are some problems with this approach. To generate a series of positive profits in all periods, it may be necessary to average over a long period, thus losing a number of initial observations.

4.4 Smoothing Data

Sales volumes and asset values of firms are subject to fluctuations due to business cycles, seasonal factors, and changes in technology and preferences. Measured as the difference between total sales and total costs, profit is moved by almost all forces on the demand and supply sides of goods and services. Business analysts and statisticians have developed a number of techniques for extracting meaningful information from volatile business time series data. One simple method is to compute moving averages for use in place of actual values. Because of the importance of smoothing data, Microsoft Excel offers a number of techniques for smoothing data mostly based on the computation of moving averages. Excel charts have options for estimating trendlines. In applications of model *FIRM*, more meaningful information may be obtained if the input data—namely, the time series of sales, capital stocks, and total costs—are smoothed before being inserted in Sheet1 of the software.

4.5   Initial or Base Year Data

The model *FIRM* developed in this book is a dynamic model that uses the data in an initial period to generate forecasts over a forecast horizon. In applications of program *FIRM* in Chap. 3, we saw that data for 2009 were used as initial data for forecasting the business variables from 2010 to 2014. As discussed in Chap. 3, abnormal profits in the base periods may underestimate or overestimate forecasts of the variables in the forecast horizon. For this reason, the model also computes normal profits in the base periods, calculates profit rate and profit margin based on the normal profits, and uses the normalized data for forecasting as shown in Sheet5.

4.6   Editing Excel Sheets

Once Excel sheets Sheet1 to Sheet6 are generated, they can be edited to produce more informative tables. For instance, in Excel Sheet2, the dollar unit of sales, costs, and capital stocks should be inserted, i.e., whether they are in $1,000 of millions of dollar. The same dollar unit should be inserted in Excel Sheet4, Sheet5, and Sheet6 for projections of sales, costs, and capital stocks. Excel options can be used to display forecasts with different numbers of digits.

4.7   The Trend Is Your Friend

For many business decisions, it is the trends in business variables that are important, rather than their exact values—for instance, whether sales level or growth rate is decreasing or increasing. Although economic models may not produce highly accurate forecasts, they can produce useful information about trends in business variables. Excel options for identifying trends in time series variables can be employed to provide information on trends in forecasts of sales, profits, capital stocks, profit rate, and profit margin generated by the business model *FIRM* presented in this book.

Finally, many forecasts can be generated using the model *FIRM* presented in this book depending on the choice of the sample periods as well as data for sales, costs, capital stocks, and profits. Over time, model users will gather more information about the forecasting accuracy of the model with different datasets and will be able to choose datasets that generate more accurate forecasts. In the end, the most important ingredient in the forecasting process is user judgment.

4.8   Error Messages

The following is a list of error messages:

1. Insufficient Number of Observations
2. Non-numeric Data in Initial Time Series Data
3. Empty Cell or Zero in Initial Time Series Data
4. Data Entry Error, Cell B7, First Year Is Empty
5. Data Entry Error, Cell B7, First Year Is Not an Integer
6. Data Entry Error, Cell B7, First Year is Not Numeric
7. Data Entry Error, Cell B8, Last Year Is Empty
8. Data Entry Error, Cell B8, Last Year Is Not an Integer
9. Data Entry Error, Cell B8, Last Year Is Not Numeric
10. Data Entry Error, Cell B8, Last Year Is Smaller Than First Year
11. Data Entry Error, Cell B9, First Quarter or First Month Is Not an Integer
12. Data Entry Error, Cell B9, First Quarter or First Month Is Empty
13. Data Entry Error, Cell B9, First Quarter or First Month is Not Numeric
14. Data Entry Error, Cell B9, First Quarter Must Be 1 to 4
15. Data Entry Error, Cell B9, First Month Must Be 1 to 12
16. Data Entry Error, Cell B10, Last Quarter or Last Month Is Not an Integer
17. Data Entry Error, Cell B10, Last Quarter or Last Month Is Empty
18. Data Entry Error, Cell B10, Last Quarter or Last Month is Not Numeric
19. Data Entry Error, Cell B10, Last Quarter Must Be 1 to 4
20. Data Entry Error, Cell B10, Last Month Must Be 1 to 12